THE ROYAL COURT THEATRE PRESENTS

BLACK SUPERHERO

by Danny Lee Wynter

BLACK SUPERHERO was first performed at the Royal Court Jerwood
Theatre Downstairs, Sloane Square, on Tuesday 14 March 2023.

BLACK SUPERHERO
by Danny Lee Wynter

Cast

Steven/Sellapath/Interviewer **Ben Allen**

King/Craw **Dyllón Burnside**

Jackson/Twink **Dominic Holmes**

Raheem **Eloka Ivo**

David **Danny Lee Wynter**

Kweku **Ako Mitchell**

Syd/Zendaya **Rochenda Sandall**

Director **Daniel Evans**
Designer **Joanna Scotcher**
Costume Designer **Kinnetia Isidore**
Lighting Designer **Ryan Day**
Sound Designer & Composer **Tingying Dong**
Video Designer **Iain Syme**
Movement Director **Gerrard Martin**
Intimacy Director **Yarit Dor**
Assistant Director **Matthew Iliffe**
Associate Costume Designer & Costume Supervisor **Zoë Thomas-Webb**
Voice and Dialect Coach **Salvatore Sorce**
US Casting Director **Victor Vazquez, CSA**
Performer flying **Lee Stephenson for Freedom Flying**
Stage Manager **Annette Waldie**
Deputy Stage Manager **Mary O'Hanlon**
Assistant Stage Manager **Tayla Hunter**
Show Crew **Oscar Sale**
Dresser **Sabirin Osman**
Design Assistants **Camille Etchart & Eve Wilson**
Costumes made by **Will Skeet, Sarah Dearing & Kingsley Hall**
Millinery by **Hannah Trickett**
Set built by **Ridiculous Solutions**
Fabric printed by **Hatley Prints**
Lighting Hires supplied by **SLX**
Marketing campaign support by **The 5th Wall**

From the Royal Court, on this production:

Casting Directors **Amy Ball & Arthur Carrington**
Stage Supervisor **TJ Chappell-Meade**
Show Crew **Maddy Collins**
Lead Producer **Sarah Georgeson**
Sound Supervisor **David McSeveney**
Production Manager **Marius Rønning**
Lighting Programmer **Stephen Settle**
Lighting Supervisor **Deanna Towli**

The Royal Court Theatre and Stage Management wish to thank the following for their help with this production: Sam Kacher, Autumn Munsell, Nick Blount, Callum Harris, Tommy Swale, Tom Glenister, Mali Bamber, Skylar Blu Copeland, Briony Berning at Ambersphere Solutions Ltd, National Theatre Sound Resources Department for loan of equipment.

Danny Lee Wynter

(Writer & David)

Danny is a playwright, Olivier-nominated actor, activist and columnist. He is the founder of Act For Change, the UK campaign group that helped change representation across the live and recorded arts.

This is Danny's debut play.

He is currently under commission to the Donmar Warehouse Theatre for his second play.

As actor:
For the Royal Court: **Living Newspaper, The Changing Room.**

Other theatre includes: **The Normal Heart** (National); Faustus: That Damned Woman (Lyric); The Maids (HOME, Manchester); Cell Mates (Hampstead); Forty Years On (Chichester Festival Theatre); Comus, Bedlam, Henry IV Part II, Henry IV Part I, King Lear, The Frontline (Globe); Deathwatch (The Print Room); The Glass Menagerie (Nuffield, Southampton); Much Ado About Nothing (Old Vic); St John's Night (Jermyn Street); The Miser (Royal Exchange, Manchester).

Television includes: **Luther, Trial and Retribution, Partners in Crime, Mr. Stink, Episodes, Walliams and Friend, Holby City.**

Film includes: **Joe's Palace & Capturing Mary, Censor, Hot Fuzz, The Dreams of Bethany Mellmouth, Beat Girl.**

Awards include: **Nominated for the Olivier Award for Best Supporting Actor (The Normal Heart).**

Ben Allen

(Steven/Sellapath/Interviewer)

Theatre includes: **Folk, Canary (& Liverpool Playhouse/ETT Tour)** (Hampstead); The Cherry Orchard, Hamlet (Theatre Royal Windsor); Gently Down The Stream (Park); Measure for Measure (Donmar); Present Laughter (Chichester Festival Theatre); Antony and Cleopatra, Julius Caesar, Oppenheimer, The Shoemaker's Holiday (Royal Shakespeare Company); The Seagull (Manchester Library Theatre Company); Twelfth Night, The Taming of the Shrew, The Merchant of Venice, The Winter's Tale, Henry V (Propeller); All's Well That Ends Well, The History Boys (National); Noises Off (Ambassador Theatre Group).

Television includes: **World On Fire, Casualty, Breeders, Soul Mates, Cursed, Doctors, Barbarians Rising, Coronation Street, Bonekickers.**

Film includes: **Another End, The Haircut, The Foreigner**

Dyllón Burnside (King/Craw)

Theatre includes: **Thoughts of a Colored Man, Holler if Ya Hear Me (Broadway), Born For This (Arena Stage), Welcome To Fear City** (Contemporary American Theatre Festival).

Television includes: **Dahmer, Pose, Prideland, American Horror Stories, High Maintenance.**

Film includes: **Wild Goat Surf, All Boys Aren't Blue, Yinz.**

Awards include: **Daytime Emmy Award for Outstanding Short Form Non Fiction Program (Prideland), Telly Award (Prideland), GLAAD Media Award (All Boys Aren't Blue).**

Ryan Day (Lighting Designer)

Theatre credits include: **Local Hero (Co-Lighting Designer with Paule Constable, Minerva – Chichester); Wild Onion (Norwich Theatre Royal/UK Tour); Lizard Boy (Hope Mill & Edinburgh Fringe); Mission, The Ballad of Corona V (The Big House); Christie Done It, Dr Faustess (Cockpit); Rabbit Hole, Darknet (Union); I Know I Know I Know (Southwark Playhouse); A Merchant of Venice (Playground Theatre); Ghost House (Vaults); Urinetown (Embassy); Attempts on Her Life (Drayton Arms); The Bexliest Day of our Lives (Exchange Erith); Primary Steps Recital (Royal Ballet School); Anatomy of a Suicide (Webber Douglas Studio).**

As associate/assistant, theatre credits include: **The Rite of Spring (Sadler's Wells/UK Tour); Wickies (Park 200); The Lemon Table (Salisbury Playhouse/UK Tour); Les Misérables, Les Misérables In Concert (Sondheim Theatre); Palmer Harding Fashion Show (Goodenough College).**

Tingying Dong

(Sound Designer & Composer)

Ting trained at LAMDA. She grew up in Beijing and studied in the Netherlands before moving to the UK.

As sound designer/composer, theatre includes: **Watch On The Rhine (Donmar); The Crucible (National, Content Sound Design); The Beekeeper of Aleppo (Nottingham Playhouse/UK Tour); My Son's A Queer (But What Can You Do?) (West End/Underbelly/Turbine); Klippies (Young Vic); After The End, The Sun, the Moon, and the Stars (Theatre Royal Stratford East); The Breach, Peggy For You, Folk (Hampstead); Scissors (Sheffield Theatres); A Christmas Carol (Nottingham Playhouse/Alexandra Palace/BBC. Composer); Antigone (Storyhouse); Ruckus (Summerhall/Southwark Playhouse); Kathy and Stella Solve a Murder (Roundabout/Francesca Moody Productions);**

Tsunagu/Connect (Shoreditch Town Hall/New Earth); Two Billion Beats (Orange Tree); Jerker (King's Head).

As creative collaborator and making sound and music, theatre includes: **Walking Cats (Camden People's/Vault Festival); Vanishing (MishMash Festival); Imaginarium (Online Tour).**

Radio composition includes: **Humane; BURP.**

Short Film composition includes: **Medea/Worn; My Last Duchess.**

Awards include: **WhatsOnStage Award for Best Off West End Production (My Son's A Queer (But What Can You Do?))**

Yarit Dor (Intimacy Director)

For the Royal Court: **That Is Not Who I Am, Purple Snowflakes, Titty Wanks (& Abbey).**

Other theatre credits include: **Rockets and Blue Lights (National); Hamilton (West End); Death of A Salesman (West End/Young Vic); The Glass Menagerie, The Shark is Broken (West End); "Daddy" A Melodrama (Almeida); The Band's Visit, Love & Other Acts of Violence (Donmar); Henry V, The Merchant of Venice, Richard II, Hamlet, As You Like It, Much Ado About Nothing (Shakespeare's Globe); Changing Destiny, Wild East (Young Vic); Old Bridge, Strange Fruit (Bush); Arms and The Man, Statements After an Arrest Under the Immorality Act, Last Easter (Orange Tree); NW Trilogy (Kiln); Scandaltown (Lyric Hammersmith); Macbeth (Royal Exchange); The Crucible, An Unfinished Man, Dirty Crusty (Yard); Miss Julie (Storyhouse); Assata Taught Me, Iphigenia Quartet (Gate); The Effect (Boulevard); The Tempest, Romeo and Juliet, As You Like It, A Midsummer Night's Dream, Tempest (Shakespeare in the Squares).**

Dance credits include: **Peaky Blinders, Rooms (Rambert Dance Company); The Burnt City (Punchdrunk); 2B, Sunday Morning, Leah, Somewhere Between A Self (Hagit Yarkira Dance).**

Film & TV credits include: **Glass Onion: Knives Out Mystery; The Colour Room; Polite Society; The Wheel Of Time; Shadow & Bone; Cheaters; Starstruck; Mood; Adult Material; Atlanta 3, SAS Rogue Heroes and Becoming Elizabeth.**

Daniel Evans (Director)

As director, theatre includes: **Our Generation (& National), Local Hero, South Pacific (& Sadler's Wells), Quiz (& Noel Coward), Fiddler on the Roof, Forty Years On (Chichester Festival Theatre); American Buffalo (Wyndham's); Show Boat (& New London), Flowers for Mrs Harris, Oliver!, My Fair Lady, Anything Goes, The Sheffield Mysteries, Macbeth, Racing Demon, Othello, An Enemy of the People, The Effect,**

This is My Family, The Full Monty (Sheffield Theatres); The Light in the Piazza (RFH/LA Opera/Chicago Lyric Opera); Esther (Theatr Genedlaethol Cymru); Lovely Evening/In The Blue (Young Vic at Theatre503).

As an actor, for the Royal Court: **Cleansed, 4.48 Psychosis, Other People, Where Do We Live?.**

As an actor, other theatre includes: **Cardiff East, Peter Pan, Candide, Troilus and Cressida, The Merchant of Venice (National); A Midsummer Night's Dream, Coriolanus, Henry V, Cymbeline, Measure For Measure (RSC); Ghosts (ETT); Merrily We Roll Along (Donmar); Sunday in the Park with George (Menier).**

Awards include: **Olivier Awards for Best Actor in a Musical (Merrily We Roll Along and Sunday in the Park with George); UK Theatre Awards for Best Musical Production (Show Boat and Flowers for Mrs Harris); WhatsOnStage Awards for Best Regional Production (Oliver! and My Fair Lady).**

Daniel is Artistic Director of Chichester Festival Theatre. Previously, he was Artistic Director of Sheffield Theatres (2009–2016). In June 2022, he will take up post as Co–Artistic Director of the Royal Shakespeare Company.

Dominic Holmes (Jackson/Twink)

Theatre includes: **Cock (Elliott & Harper); Vincent River (Hope Mill); Henry IV (Waterloo East/ Ivy Arts Centre); Macbeth (Out of Joint).**

Television includes: **Hullraisers, F U Martin Parker, Industry, War of the Worlds, Two Weeks to Live, Jinx, Coronation Street, Heartbeat.**

Film includes: **Role Play.**

Tayla Hunter
(Assistant Stage Manager)

As company stage manager: **imaginary natural beings (Vaults).**

As assistant stage manager: **Paradise Now!, The P Word (Bush); Lotus Beauty (Hampstead); A Place for We (Park/Talawa).**

Awards include: **Offie for Best Ensemble (A Place for We).**

Matthew Iliffe (Assistant Director)

As director: **Bacon, The Niceties, Maggie May (Finborough); Four Play (Above The Stag); The Burnt Part Boys (Park Theatre).**

As assistant/associate director: **Assassins (Chichester Festival Theatre); Musik (Leicester Square Theatre); A Midsummer Night's Dream**

(National Tour, Changeling Theatre Company); Romeo & Juliet (Site-Responsive, Insane Root Theatre Company); Brass (Hackney Empire, National Youth Music Theatre).

Awards include: **Off-West End Award for Best Director (Bacon).**

Matthew graduated from the University of Bristol with a first-class honours' degree in Theatre & Performance Studies and trained as a director on the StoneCrabs Young Directors Programme at The Albany, Deptford.

Kinnetia Isidore (Costume Designer)

As costume designer, theatre credits: **Adult Children (Donmar); Our Generation (National, The Minerva Chichester); Jesus Hopped the 'A' Train (Young Vic); The Wife of Willesden (co-designer); Kiln, Brooklyn Academy of Music, American Repertory Theater Boston); Enter Achilles (Rambert, Sadler's Wells & Onassis Stegi), Scandaltown, Aladdin (Lyric Hammersmith); The Night Woman (The Other Palace).**

As associate costume designer, theatre credits: **Constellations (Donmar, Vaudeville West End); Ragtime (ArtsEd); Lemons, Lemons, Lemons, Lemons, Lemons (Harold Pinter West End).**

Eloka Ivo (Raheem)

Theatre includes: **The Glass Menagerie (Royal Exchange); The Gods Are Not to Blame (Almeida); The End of Eddy (BAM New York); One Night in Miami (Bristol Old Vic/Nottingham Playhouse); The Son (Kiln); To Kill a Mockingbird (Lyric); Victoria's Knickers (Soho Theatre).**

Television includes: **Avenue 5.**

Film includes: **Four Mothers.**

Gerrard Martin

(Movement Director)

As movement director: **Shepard's Chameleon (Utopia Theatre); Lady Macwata (Ghost light Theatre); GHB Boy (Charing Cross Theatre); BEAM (Britten Arts); CAKE (Theatre Peckham); 60 Miles by Road or Rail (Royal & Derngate); Foxes (Theatre503); The Frontline (CSSD).**

As choreographer: **Tate Modern, The Place, Curve Theatre, National Portrait Gallery, South Bank, British Museum, National Portrait Gallery and The West Bengal Federation of Dance, India and the Athens Video Dance Project, Greece.**

As assistant choreographer: **Porgy and Bess (English National Opera); One Love Musical (Birmingham Rep); the 40th UAE Royal**

Anniversary Performance, Abu Dhabi (Generating Company).
As dance teacher: **The Place, Mountview Academy of Theatre Arts, Dance Works, Royal Central School of Speech and Drama and the Royal Academy of Dramatic Art.**

As dancer for companies and organisations: **Phoenix Dance Company, Tavaziva Dance, Union Dance Company and Ballet Black, The Lion King, Aletta Collins Dance Company, State of Emergency, National Theatre, English National Opera, Royal Opera House.**

Gerrard is a performer, choreographer, movement director, dance educator, yoga teacher and consultant. He created a project-based company Gerrard Martin Dance (GMD) in 2011 which produces works of emotive and socially relevant dance-theatre; to teach and facilitate creativity through movement, yoga, and dance. Gerrard is the co-founder of Black Artists in Dance, (BAiD); whose mission is to create a physical and digital platform that responds to the educational and professional needs of those working within the dance industry. To showcase the contribution that black dancers, artists and academics make to the development of dance, specifically within the UK as a means to enrich the dance sector.

Ako Mitchell (Kweku)

Theatre includes: **The Light In The Piazza (Alexandra Palace); The Color Purple (Leicester Curve/Birmingham Hippodrome & UK National Tour); Chess (Theatre Royal Drury Lane); Bonnie & Clyde (Arts Theatre, West End); Indecent Proposal, Grey Gardens (Southwark); Bernstein's Wonderful Town (Opera Holland Park); Far From Heaven (MTFest 2021); Europa Projekt Season: Europeana and Peer Gynt (RSC); Caroline, Or Change (Chichester, Hampstead and West End); Guys And Dolls, Little Shop of Horrors (Manchester Royal Exchange); The Wild Party (The Other Palace); Ragtime (Charing Cross); The Trial Of Jane Fonda, Klook's Last Stand (Park); Misanthropes (Old Vic New Voices); How To Succeed In Business Without Really Trying (Royal Festival Hall); Fences (Duchess); The 25th Annual Putnam County Spelling Bee (Donmar); Sweaty Eddie in Sister Act (London Palladium); Mufasa in The Lion King (Lyceum); The Mystery Plays (Bath Music Festival); Broadway in the Shadows (Luxembourg National Theatre and Arcola).**

Television credits include: **FBI: International, The Grinch That Stole Christmas, Hilda, Gameface, Avenue 5, Best & Bester, Silent Witness, Berlin Station.**

Film includes: **Marvel's Doctor Strange in the Multiverse of Madness, Daddy's Head, The Lion Vs The Little People, Lake Placid: The Final Chapter, Johnny English Strikes Again.**

Ako directed and co-wrote the short I'm in the corner with the bluebells which premiered at the Toronto International Film Festival and won Best Director at the Mica Film Festival in Brazil.

Ako also wrote and directed the short I Promise –winner of the Cineuropa Shorts / Filminute Audience Award.

Radio includes: **Mueller: Trump Tower Moscow, Strangest Weather on Earth.**

Mary O'Hanlon

(Deputy Stage Manager)

For the Royal Court: **Belong.**

Theatre includes: **Mandela, The Collaboration, Changing Destiny, Tree, Twelfth Night** (Young Vic); **Legally Blonde** (Regent's Park); **The Mountaintop** (Royal Exchange, Manchester/Prism/National Tour); **Glengarry Glen Ross** (National Tour); **Hamlet/As You Like It** (Globe); **The Treatment** (Almeida); **One Night In Miami...,** **Faith Healer, Closer, The Same Deep Water As Me, Richard II, King Lear** (& UK tour/BAM NY); **King Lear, The Late Middle Classes, Serenading Louis** (& UK tour); **A Doll's House, Four Quartets, The Family Reunion** (Donmar); **Much Ado About Nothing** (Globe/UK and European Tour/South and North America Tour); **Solid Air** (Theatre Royal, Plymouth); **Paper Dolls, Red Velvet** (Tricycle); **Design for Living** (Old Vic); **One Step Forward, One Step Back** (dreamthinkspeak–Liverpool Cathedral); **Shadowlands, The Hound of the Baskervilles, The Snowman** (West End); **Tristan and Yseult** (UK Tour/Spoleto Festival South Carolina), **Cymbeline** (RSC/UK Tour/Kneehigh); **South Pacific, Free, The Shadow of a Boy, Sanctuary** (& UK tour), **Henry V, Edmond, Falstaff, His Dark Materials, Iphigenia at Aulis, The History Boys, A Dream Play, The President of an Empty Room, ...some trace of her** (National); **Pericles** (Ludlow Festival).

TV credits include: **CBeebies: Dick Whittington and His Cat, CBeebies presents: As You Like It, Play In A Day.**

Rochenda Sandall (Syd/Zendaya)

For the Royal Court: **Maryland, Gundog.**

Other theatre includes: **Talking Heads – The Outside Dog** (Bridge); **The Playroom** (Young Vic); **The Nap** (Sheffield Crucible); **Pomona** (& Manchester Royal Exchange), **Scenes from an Execution** (National); **Little Malcolm and his Struggle Against the Eunuchs** (Southwark); **Coriolanus** (Donmar). Television includes: **The Rig, Great Expectations, Doctor Who, Deceit, Small Axe, Talking Heads – The Outside Dog, Line of Duty S5, Unprecedented, Criminal, Black Mirror.**

Film includes: **Star Wars – The Rise of Skywalker, Bufflehead.**

Radio includes: **Lady Macbeth of Mtsensk.**

Joanna Scotcher (Designer)

For the Royal Court: **Cuttin' It** (& Young Vic/Birmingham Rep/Sheffield Theatres), **Pests** (& Clean Break/Royal Exchange).

Other theatre includes: **The Vortex, Doubt: A Parable, Sing Yer Heart Out For The Lads** (Chichester Festival Theatre); **Macbeth** (Almeida); **Fantastically Great Women Who Changed The World** (Theatre Royal Stratford East / UK Tour); **Women Beware Women, Emilia** (& West End) (Globe); **Love, Love, Love** (Lyric Hammersmith); **Mother Courage, Anna Karenina, The Rolling Stone** (Royal Exchange/Headlong); **The Village** (Theatre Royal Stratford East); **Winter, Two Endless Moments, A Harlem Dream** (Young Vic); **Katie Roche** (Abbey, Dublin); **Boys Will Be Boys** (Bush/Headlong); **The Railway Children** (Kings Cross Theatre/Waterloo/Toronto).

Opera as designer includes: **She Described It To Death, Current Rising** (Royal Opera House)

Awards include: **Olivier for Best Costume Design (Emilia), WhatsOnStage Award for Best Set Designer (The Railway Children).**

Salvatore Sorce

(Voice and Dialect Coach)

Theatre includes: **A Little Life** (Harold Pinter Theatre); **The Two Popes** (UK Tour); **Girl from the North Country** (UK tour); **Bad Jews** (Arts Theatre); **First Touch** (Nottingham Playhouse); **Persuasion** (Rose Theatre, Kingston and UK tour); **Best of Enemies** (Young Vic); **Romeo and Juliet, Eyam** (Shakespeare's Globe); **Goodnight Mr Tom** (Duke of York's).

Television includes: **My Lady Jane; Transatlantic, The Toys that Built America, Desperate Measures, Devil's Advocate, Then Barbara Met Alan, Grinch: The Musical, Don't Forget the Driver.**

Film includes: **Silver, A Bit of Light.**

Zoë Thomas–Webb

(Associate Costume Designer & Costume Supervisor)

As associate: **Lessons in Love and Violence** (Liceu Opera Barcelona).

As costume supervisor: **Sleeping Beauty** (New Adventures); **Blue Woman** (Royal Opera House); **Oklahoma, Best of Enemies** (The Young Vic); **The 47th** (Old Vic).

Annette Waldie (Stage Manager)

As company stage manager: **Heart Of Hammersmith (Lyric Hammersmith); Losing Venice (Orange Tree).**

As CSM on the Book: **Rain and Zoe Save the World (Jermyn Street Theatre); Rapunzel (Chipping Norton Theatre); The Jumper Factory (Young Vic); Reared (Bold); In Event of Moone Disaster (Theatre503).**

As deputy stage manager: **2022 Mischief Festival (RSC); Cinderella (Stephen Joseph Theatre); Utility (Orange Tree).**

As assistant stage manager: **2018–2020 Summer season and National Tour (RSC); Salomé (National).**

THE ROYAL COURT THEATRE

The Royal Court Theatre is the writers' theatre. It is a leading force in world theatre for cultivating and supporting writers – undiscovered, emerging and established.

Through the writers, the Royal Court is at the forefront of creating restless, alert, provocative theatre about now. We open our doors to the unheard voices and free thinkers that, through their writing, change our way of seeing.

Over 120,000 people visit the Royal Court in Sloane Square, London, each year and many thousands more see our work elsewhere through transfers to the West End and New York, UK and international tours, digital platforms, our residencies across London, and our site-specific work. Through all our work we strive to inspire audiences and influence future writers with radical thinking and provocative discussion.

The Royal Court's extensive development activity encompasses a diverse range of writers and artists and includes an ongoing programme of writers' attachments, readings, workshops and playwriting groups. Twenty years of the International Department's pioneering work around the world means the Royal Court has relationships with writers on every continent.

Since 1956 we have commissioned and produced hundreds of writers, from John Osborne to Jasmine Lee-Jones. Royal Court plays from every decade are now performed on stage and taught in classrooms and universities across the globe.

We strive to create an environment in which differing voices and opinions can co-exist. In current times, it is becoming increasingly difficult for writers to write what they want or need to write without fear, and we will do everything we can to rise above a narrowing of viewpoints.

It is because of this commitment to the writer and our future that we believe there is no more important theatre in the world than the Royal Court.

Supported using public funding by
ARTS COUNCIL ENGLAND

ARTS COUNCIL ENGLAND

royalcourt royalcourttheatre

ROYAL

ASSISTED PERFORMANCES

Captioned Performances

Captioned performances are accessible for people who are D/deaf, deafened & hard of hearing, as well as being suitable for people for whom English is not a first language.

BLACK SUPERHERO: 12, 19 April 7:30pm, 27 April 2:30pm

BSL-interpreted Performances

BSL-interpreted performances, delivered by an interpreter, give a sign inteprretation of the text spoken and/or sung by artists in the onstage production.

COURT

ROYAL

ASSISTED PERFORMANCES

Performances in a Relaxed Environment

Relaxed Environment performances are suitable for those who may benefit from a more relaxed environment.

During these performances:
- There is a relaxed attitude to noise in the auditorium; you are welcome to respond to the show in whatever way feels natural
- You can enter and exit the auditorium when needed
- We will help you find the best seats for your experience
- House lights may remain raised slightly
- Loud noises may be reduced

BLACK SUPERHERO: 22 April 2:30pm

If you would like to talk to us about your access requirements, please contact our Box Office at (0)20 7565 5000 or boxoffice@royalcourttheatre.com
The Royal Court Visual Story is available on our website. Story and Sensory synposes are available on the show pages via the Whats On tab of the website shortly after Press Night.

COURT

ROYAL COURT SUPPORTERS

Our incredible community of supporters makes it possible for us to achieve our mission of nurturing and platforming writers at every stage of their careers. Our supporters are part of our essential fabric – they help to give us the freedom to take bigger and bolder risks in our work, develop and empower new voices, and create world–class theatre that challenges and disrupts the theatre ecology.

To all our supporters, thank you. You help us to write the future.

ROYAL

BAR & KITCHEN

The Royal Court's Bar & Kitchen aims to create a welcoming and inspiring environment with a style and ethos that reflects the work we put on stage.

Offering expertly crafted cocktails alongside an extensive selection of craft gins and beers, wine and soft drinks, our vibrant basement bar provides a sanctuary in the middle of Sloane Square. By day a perfect spot for meetings or quiet reflection and by night atmospheric meeting spaces for cast, crew, audiences and the general public.

All profits go directly to supporting the work of the Royal Court theatre, cultivating and supporting writers – undiscovered, emerging and established.

For more information, visit
royalcourttheatre.com/bar

HIRES & EVENTS

The Royal Court is available to hire for celebrations, rehearsals, meetings, filming, ceremonies and much more. Our two theatre spaces can be hired for conferences and showcases, and the building is a unique venue for bespoke events and receptions.

For more information, visit
royalcourttheatre.com/events

Sloane Square London, SW1W 8AS ⊖ Sloane Square ⇌ Victoria Station
🐦 royalcourt f theroyalcourttheatre ◉ royalcourttheatre

COURT

SUPPORT THE COURT AND BE A PART OF OUR FUTURE.

Every penny raised goes directly towards producing bold new writing for our stages, cultivating and supporting writers in the UK and around the world, and inspiring the next generation of theatre-makers.

You can make a one-off donation by text:

Text **Support 5** to 70560 to donate £5
Text **Support 10** to 70560 to donate £10
Text **Support 20** to 70560 to donate £20

Texts cost the donation amount plus one standard message. UK networks only.

To find out more about the different ways in which you can get involved, visit our website: royalcourttheatre.com/support-us

The English Stage Company at the Royal Court Theatre is a registered charity (No.231242)

BLACK SUPERHERO

Danny Lee Wynter

For Liberty

Acknowledgements

I'd like to thank, as mentioned, our creative team and company, and also:

Vicky Featherstone, Noma Dumezweni, Dominic Cooke, Sinead Matthews, Jodie McNee, Jonathan Harvey, Mel Kenyon, Rachel Taylor, Hugh Skinner, Jennifer Matter, Anthony Blunn, Ajamu X, Pearl Chanda, Nikki Amuka-Bird, John Donnelly, Richard Atwill, Martina Laird, Christopher Shinn, Luke Norris, Kobna Holdbrook-Smith, Samuel Adamson, Sarah Georgeson, Jane Fallowfield, Anthony Simpson-Pike, Franc Ashman, Gabriel Bisset-Smith, Chris Campbell, Amy Ball, Arthur Carrington, Victor Vasquez, Ultz, Giles Terera, Matt Applewhite, Chandra Ruegg, Danielle Chen, Tom McKay, Deborah Parry, Celia Wright, Jeremy O. Harris, Vicki Mortimer, David Eldridge, Kingsley Ben-Adir, Susan Wokoma, Benjamin McCann, Michael Longhurst, Cyril Nri, Stefan Adegbola, Kyle Beltran, Tyler-Jo Richardson, David Judge, Saffron Coomber, Christian Coulson, Griffin Matthews, Matthew Iliffe, Stuart Thompson, Fisayo Akinade, Alastair Coomer, Steven Webb, Don Gilet, and finally, Daniel Evans, who told me to go to drama school, then twenty years later willed me to the finish line of this play.

DLW, London,
March 2023

'…Idols are meant to be destroyed'

From the 1961 essay 'Alas, Poor Richard'
by James Baldwin

Characters

1   DAVID, *late thirties, mixed race*

2   KING, *mid- to late thirties, black or mixed race*
    CRAW, *a superhero*

3   SYD, *mid- to late thirties, mixed race*
    ZENDAYA, *a superhero*
    HOST, *mid-thirties, mixed race*

4   RAHEEM, *mid- to late thirties, black*

5   KWEKU, *mid-fifties, black*

6   STEVEN, *late thirties, white*
    SELLAPATH, *a superhero*
    ROOM SERVICE, *mid-thirties, white*
    INTERVIEWER, *late thirties, white*

7   JACKSON, *mid-twenties, white*
    TWINK, *late twenties, white*

This text went to press before the end of rehearsals and so may differ slightly from the play as performed.

ACT ONE

Scene One

RAHEEM	Chris O'Donnell. Chris O'Donnell in *Batman Forever* made me a fag.
SYD	What's up?
RAHEEM	I wanted him to do *very* bad things.
KING	He said you never touch me the way you touched Raheem, then he left.
RAHEEM	What do you mean left?
SYD	I get jealous of Jake's friends.
DAVID	That's cos they're all fetuses.
SYD	(*Giving* DAVID *the finger.*) Go fuck yerself.
RAHEEM	We've not seen David in how long? We organise this night, a night we can all be together and Stevie, what, ups and leaves cos you touched my arm?
KING	I think he thought it looked intimate.
RAHEEM	Friends *are* intimate!
DAVID	To a point.
KING	We have an open marriage.
	A beat.
RAHEEM	Since?
KING	Arizona.
SYD	And you're only tellin us now?!
	A beat.
	He met someone, he met someone, he's glowin, I can tell.

RAHEEM	What's his name?
KING	Don.
SYD	Don?
RAHEEM	Gay or straight?
KING	Gay.
RAHEEM	Good. Ain't nothin more depressin than a gay pining over a straight.
KING	He's a musician.
SYD	How old?
KING	Twenty-two.
RAHEEM	Twenty-two?!!
SYD	Oh my days, *so* Madonna.
KING	We met on this job.
RAHEEM	What job?
KING	Arizona. Technically it was Albuquerque. He played the brother of my love interest.
SYD	Your straight love interest.
DAVID	They let him play anythin.
RAHEEM	Only cos he can!
SYD	Hold up, hold up there Mr Lover Lover, hold up. You say he's called Don? He's a musician – and he acts – and he's called Don?
KING	That's correct.
SYD	Is my bredrin stickin it to Donald Glover?
KING	He's from Hounslow.
SYD	Donald Glover ain't from Hounslow.
KING	But *my* Don, *my* Don, he's from Hounslow.
SYD	*My* Don, / my Don!

KING	He made me feel young, y'all.
RAHEEM	You *are* young, brother King!
KING	No, I mean *real* young. Young like when I was a kid.
DAVID	And Stevie knows?
KING	I came home, told him everythin.
SYD	*Everythin*?
KING	*Everythin*. It doesn't change how I feel. He's still my partner. I love him. But we realised if we want it to work, and we *do* want it to work, then we have to be open.
DAVID	Well.
KING	You always say that.
DAVID	Say what?
KING	When you don't wanna say what you're really thinkin you just go well.
DAVID	Oh... Well.
	KING *shoots him a look*.
KING	I better make sure he's okay.
	He goes.
SYD	Fuck me!
RAHEEM	Technically he now can.
SYD	BOYS, BOYS, BOYS!
RAHEEM	What?
SYD	Well, King gets ding-dong, Stevie gets none.
RAHEEM	What you chattin about? Stevie can get ding-dong if he wants ding-dong.
DAVID	Not if there's no ding-dong on offer.
RAHEEM	Meaning?

DAVID	Meaning, King's a superhero! He's got fans as far as North Korea travellin halfway across the continent to declare their undyin love.
RAHEEM	And?
DAVID	And Stevie's a travel writer from Ealing, plus the most boring white man yer ever likely to meet.
RAHEEM	What goes on in someone's relationship's up to them.
DAVID	This is why straights didn't want us to marry.
SYD	If my Jake asked me I couldn't.
RAHEEM	How d'ya know if ya ain't ever tried?
DAVID	Heard you both at it again last night.
SYD	What can I say. He's twenty-nine and in his prime. I'm thirty-seven and in mine.
DAVID	Jesus.
SYD	The sex is tasty bro, it's very very tasty. I make no apologies.
DAVID	I ain't askin for an apology, just shuttin the door'll do.
RAHEEM	I'm gettin another bottle of prosecco... We're gettin fucked!

Something like 'Point and Kill' by Little Simz & Obongjayar plays.

Scene Two

SYD	We did this kids party last week. Nottin Hill. I was Princess Elsa.
DAVID	Uber's comin.
SYD	This kid comes up to me, he goes Princess Elsa's not black.
RAHEEM	Who?
SYD	This kid, the one I'm tellin you about. Fat fuck. Chunk from *The Goonies*.
DAVID	You can't say that. Even if you think it you can't say it.
RAHEEM	For me it was always Corey Feldman.
SYD	He had a poster of him on his bedroom wall. Used to bash one out over it.
DAVID	Nasty.
SYD	That or the underwear models in Mum's Next catalogue.
RAHEEM	It was always Littlewoods for us.
	SYD *observing* RAHEEM*'s physique*.
SYD	Oi oi, Princess Muscles.
RAHEEM	New job innit.
	DAVID *locates the Uber.*
	Gotta keep meself nice and tight. And, check this.
	RAHEEM *holds out his phone, they stare*.
SYD	Oh my, he is a real one. Becky with the good glutes.
RAHEEM	French.
DAVID	Where'd ya find him?

RAHEEM	We met one summer sheep herding in the Wyoming mountains.
	DAVID *unimpressed*.
	Raya. I joined, they didn't believe it was me bruv.
DAVID	Two films suddenly she's Jennifer Lawrence.
RAHEEM	Then you won't be wantin one of my exclusive friendship passes.
DAVID	You reckon they'll 'ave me?
RAHEEM	If they hear you're friends with us I'm sure they'll consider.
DAVID	(*His phone pings, he looks*.) Cancelled.
SYD	FUCK'S SAKE!
RAHEEM	(*As he goes*.) I'm takin a leak.
	SYD *has lost something*. DAVID *picks up her cardigan, hands it to her. She puts it on and curls up in his lap. After a while* SYD *imitates Tiffany Pollard on* Celebrity Big Brother –
SYD	I would let Gemma know that she is a / fat cunt
DAVID	Fat cunt
SYD	And, um / the shoes that she gave me were not somethin that I would particularly buy for myself. They were old-maiden type of shoes... She was unqualified to own those shoes.
DAVID	The shoes that she gave me were not somethin that I would particularly buy for myself... old-maiden type of shoes.
	Pause.
	Why d'ya think Stevie came tonight? He never usually does...
	A beat.

Maybe he don't trust King no more… Or maybe…

He looks down at SYD. *She has fallen asleep.* KING *enters.*

KING   (*With a smile.*) I got ambushed. (*Moving to* DAVID.) Does my breath smell?

He breathes out. DAVID *smells it.*

DAVID   Nah.

KING   Stevie hates it when I smoke. Says it's a sign of weakness.

DAVID   You ain't weak. You're the mighty Craw from Crawtopia, remember?

A TWINK *approaches.*

TWINK   I'm sorry to ask, but are you King Grant?

KING   (*MLE accent.*) Who's askin?

TWINK   You look like him.

KING   Sorry… (*Smiling with complete charm, as himself.*) I'm playin witchu.

TWINK   I knew it. Oh my God. Mind if I get a selfie?

KING   Sure.

The TWINK *hands* DAVID *his phone.* DAVID *untangles from* SYD.

TWINK   Mate, you were so *so* good in *Craw Control.* You bodied it! *Bodied* it!

KING drapes his arm over TWINK, DAVID *takes the selfie.*

My little brother idolises you. Thinks you're an actual superhero.

DAVID   (*Handing the phone back.*) He is.

KING   Filter it to fuck.

	TWINK *looks at the selfie, smiles, then turns to* DAVID.
TWINK	This, *this* is a good friend to 'ave.
	He turns and does the salute.
	Crawtopia in Excelsis!
KING	(*With a quiet reluctance, returning the salute.*) Crawtopia in Excelsis!
	TWINK *goes off.* KING *and* DAVID *look at each other.*
DAVID	You guys alright?
KING	You mean Stevie? He hasn't replied... I better go.
DAVID	Fancy the Turner exhibition next week?
KING	Yeah. Let me take you. My treat.
	He downs his pint.
	How's the new job?
DAVID	One of the dads tried to cop off with me.
KING	Was he fine?
DAVID	Mmm. Ish... I was dressed as Peppa Pig at the time so I weren't really feelin it.
	KING *laughs.*
	I ain't an actor now, I'm a clown. (*A little maudlin.*) I mean, what am I doin with my life? Workin for my little sister.
KING	Why you *always* put yourself down like that?
	A beat.
DAVID	What? You gunna tell me it gets better? S'wha my therapist says.
KING	I don't think it does get better. *You* on the other hand, *you* get better... If you want to, that is.

DAVID *looks at him.*

What's that thing Voltaire said? He said we get this little patch of land and it's up to us to water it. That we gotta dig in our own garden. *That's* what you're doin... It'll be fine.

KING *playfully hits* DAVID*'s shoulder and smiles.*

Craw from Crawtopia never lies, remember? One of my superpowers.

Something like 'Trapped' by Colonel Abrams takes us into –

Scene Three

RAHEEM	The guy they offered the part to, he dropped out. He said it was *unconscionable* to take a gay role from a gay actor, blah, blah.
DAVID	You don't believe in that argument.
RAHEEM	Someone's gotta play the part, might as well be me.
DAVID	Didn't you once say gays playin gays was reductive?
RAHEEM	(*To* KING). I'm gonna go back in.
DAVID	(*Laughing.*) Did you or did you *not* say that?
RAHEEM	(*Turning to go.*) Yup, I'm goin in.
DAVID	When Darren Criss said he'd no longer play gay you called him an arsehole.
RAHEEM	Actually I called him a motherfuckin arsehole, but only cos he waited, he specifically waited till he got like the

	Streisand of all gay parts that would change his career forever, then the sanctimonious prick decides, what, suddenly he's got principles?
DAVID	People are allowed to change their minds!
RAHEEM	Oh hi there virtue signallin, hi.
DAVID	So in that interview you did last week?
RAHEEM	I knew ya motherfucker was gunna bring / this up, didn't I say he'd bring it up?
DAVID	You didn't say a word, not a word for the community. Best person for the job?
RAHEEM	What ya gettin at?
DAVID	Best person rarely means best person, just what six or seven names make the list!
RAHEEM	I'm an actor, David, not an activist. Activism's what you do. Sorry, *did*.
DAVID	Only cos I saw a direct link between why I weren't workin and white supremacy.
RAHEEM	(*Sending him up*.) Oh, Miss Angelou, such a martyr for the cause.
DAVID	I READ THAT INTERVIEW!
RAHEEM	Stop raisin your voice.
DAVID	I read that interview and I couldn't help but feel – well... I was disappointed.
RAHEEM	Why? Cos I don't wanna be pigeonholed, / what's your problem?
DAVID	No. Cos you're black and have a platform yet rarely use it.
RAHEEM	Bein black shouldn't enslave me to being a role model. Fuck that. What?

DAVID *mutters something under his breath.*

We not seen you in how long? Why you always blame me for my success?

DAVID   I do not blame you / for your success.

RAHEEM   Wha's tha about? Cos I don't think / it's about me.

DAVID   (*Calmly.*) When they asked where you stood in the fight for gays playin gays you said '*Best actor for the job*,' as if it didn't affect *any* of us out here in the community.

RAHEEM   Community? Community, there is no fuckin community!

DAVID   Course there's a community!

RAHEEM   Starbucks and their rainbow cups once a year? There ain't been a real community in years, bruv.

DAVID   You wilfully misinterpret.

RAHEEM   So lesbians, drag queens and transsexuals all broke a heel in Stonewall for what? A bunch of rich gays who jump on the London-to-Brighton train each year to get fucked up on MDMA? Is *this* the community yer referrin to?

KING   (*To himself.*) I enjoyed that day.

RAHEEM   I know you had a tough year Dave, but Jeez.

KING   Come, we're friends.

RAHEEM   I won't apologise for havin a career!

DAVID   Your career ain't the issue, it's ya beliefs.

          RAHEEM *looks away.*

          For years if we wanted a career we had to be so far at the back of the closet we were in fuckin Narnia! Straights took those parts, *they* cleaned up! So after *all that* what's wrong with us gettin more opportunity to play

	ourselves in our *own* stories? And as black gay men WHERE THE FUCK ARE OUR STORIES? Where're our parts?
RAHEEM	Why's it always about race with you? All the time, *race*, *race*, *race*. It's borin.
DAVID	Oh my days.
RAHEEM	This over-fixation with black culture, everyone's over-fixation with black culture.
DAVID	You really think you're bein offered these roles on merit alone?
RAHEEM	In a lot of black actors' cases no... but in mine – *yes*!
DAVID	Black people'll only be free when *all* black people are free. Not jus the lucky few who depend on the work of the many.
RAHEEM	I've 'ad enough of this Ava DuVernay outreach shit, I'm goin in.
DAVID	(*To stop him.*) You're ashamed.
RAHEEM	Huh?
DAVID	You're ashamed of who you are.
RAHEEM	Ooh eee you wanna fuckin fuck the fuck outta my face, no really, just / get him outta my face, outta my face, GET THE FUCK OUT OF MY FACE, y'know nothin, NOTHIN, nothin about nothin, that's what he knows.
DAVID	Then why, why can't you talk, like really *really* talk about bein a big black faggot when interviewed on TV or on the podcasts. You can't. You can't. You jus – you can't.
RAHEEM	Listen to yaself, fam. Stand there policin my thoughts, my opinions. Reckon yer bringin about equality tellin others what is and isn't acceptable? I ain't defined by my blackness, or my gayness.

	DAVID *looks at him.*
	WHAT?
	DAVID *laughs.*
	Why you laughin? WHY THE FUCK'S HE LAUGHIN?
DAVID	Cos in a society designed to benefit white people, still controlled by white people –
RAHEEM	This is dry, this is fuckin, / this is dry, so dry –
DAVID	You're absolutely defined by your blackness *and* gayness, and it's pure ego, *EGO* to stand there suggestin otherwise. We're defined by the choices of white people on the daily. Don't you ever think it might be nice to give somethin back? To raise people up?
RAHEEM	I raise people up. I raise people up all the time!
DAVID	Who?
RAHEEM	Erm. People of colour. Women. My sisters. I'm a raiser! I'm a fuckin raiser! I mean, I jus offered you the opportunity to go on Raya. (*He smiles.*) I'm good people.
DAVID	But in that interview –
	RAHEEM *losing his shit.*
RAHEEM	FUCK THE INTERVIEW!
DAVID	I'm just sayin.
RAHEEM	You're not just sayin, yer fuckin judgin. You did it tonight with him!
	He gestures wildly to KING.
	Does he or does he not get to have sex outside marriage? It's none of your fuckin business! And sis, you're the last person who should be judgin anyone. Truss.

KING	Chill.
RAHEEM	This Goody Two-Shoes act don't fool us, Hermione. I known you from time.

No one says anything.

Fuck this. I'm out.

He exits.

KING	I think he might be upset.
DAVID	(*Quickly.*) Fuck him!
KING	You don't mean –
DAVID	Nah. Nah, fuck him. I'm done with gays not supportin other gays, then idiots like that spoutin '*artistic licence*'.

KING *goes to interject, but –*

He's now a beneficiary of an equality he don't even believe in. And for what? So he can be some paid-partnership poof on the 'gram?... I notice you didn't say anythin.

KING	Now's not the time.
DAVID	When is?
KING	You think I'm a bad person.
DAVID	I didn't say a word.
KING	Didn't have to.

DAVID *looks away.*

Stevie and I fight all the time now. We make up, we argue again, and so it goes on.

KING *fiddles with his wedding ring.*

I go off on this press tour next month. Stevie can't come. When he told me I was relieved. Does that make me sound bad?

A beat.

There was this moment. Couple of years ago. You and I we were in a cab goin through forget where. Stevie was away. We'd just moved into the house. I said don't go back to yours. I offered you the couch.

A beat.

I think I was sort of sayin…

DAVID   Sort of sayin what?

KING   I was sort of sayin…

He places his hand on the top of DAVID*'s thigh.*

DAVID   Oh.

KING   Janelle Monáe. The Roundhouse. We lost Stevie in the crowd… I can be home chillin, something'll come on the radio… What's David think of that? (*He looks at* DAVID.) There were other times too.

DAVID   Why didn't you say?

KING   I was with Stevie.

DAVID   You *are* with Stevie!

KING   Yeah, only now it's open. Now I'm completely honest. I don't feel like oh, I can't look at anyone, or, oh I can't find someone attractive. Even friends. (*Like a child with excitement.*) I'm just sorta goin *yeah*. So is Stevie. I don't feel so racked with guilt about it now, whereas before… For right or wrong I'm sayin yes.

Pause.

What?

DAVID   You and Raheem. Everythin you touch, platinum gold, jus like that. People wanna be around it cos it makes em feel good. *You* make

	em feel good. Good about emselves, good about the world. It's like bein friends with the Holy fuckin Grail. And you're good! Like *really* good! And young, and vital, and handsome, and rich... Yer in ya prime.
KING	You're in your prime too, silly.
DAVID	I had a dream once of playin Hamlet. Next week I'm auditionin for Horatio.
KING	What's wrong with Horatio?
DAVID	I don't wanna play Horatio, thank you very much... do you?

Something like 'Fuck Him All Night' by Azealia Banks begins playing from inside.

I'm thirty-nine. I live with my kid sister and her partner who I've nothin in common with. I'm talkin like zero... They're tryin for a baby. Asked me to move out. But if I move I gotta get a deposit. And if I ain't got no deposit I can't move. It's heavy, y'know. It's like, it's really *really* heavy... I didn't think –

KING *quickly kisses* DAVID. *Once. Twice. A third time in a sort of fury.* RAHEEM *appears.*

RAHEEM	Don't mind me.

DAVID *suddenly breaks away.*

I met a pole-dancin twink in the toilet who wants to take me to Heaven.

KING	...Are you gunna let him?
RAHEEM	He's got guest list for Adonis... I might.

KING *holds his hand out. Perhaps* RAHEEM *dances towards them. Perhaps* KING *joins in. After* KING *takes hold of* RAHEEM*'s hand, pulls him in and kisses him.* DAVID *watches.*

Rude.

KING *now turns to* DAVID, *he kisses him too.*

Very... very... rude.

KING *shares them back and forth until he decides to break it. The three men holding each other now laugh. The kissing and groping becomes more bacchanalian as the music from within swells into the night.*

Scene Four

DAVID *and* KING *lay naked. After a while the phone rings.* KING *suddenly bolts up, fumbles about, finds it and switches it to vibrate.* DAVID *rolls over. He looks at him.*

KING	Where are we?
DAVID	Shoreditch. You told the cabby to take us to a motel.
	KING *lays back, puts on some music. Something like 'I Know What You Want' by Busta Rhymes and Mariah Carey feat. The Flipmode Squad.*
KING	Raheem.
DAVID	You wanted him too. You wanted us both... What do you think Stevie'll say?
KING	It's fine, we're open.
DAVID	Yeah, but not to the likes of me.
KING	The likes of –
DAVID	Not with someone he's always known has...
KING	Always known what?
	DAVID *doesn't answer.*

I didn't mean to drag you into my mess. Oh my
God, what a twat.

KING *smiles his mega-watt smile.*

I enjoyed it... Last night... Am I allowed to
say that?

They listen to music.

When I got married I thought that would be
that. We fought for the rights. Won them. It all
happened rather quick. Suddenly Stevie's got
us a wedding list at John Lewis. No one in my
family ever got married. Not one.

A beat.

I'm unable to offer him a way back. I have to
explore these feelings. I can't lie.

*Silence. KING lip-syncs to the song. DAVID,
still in his arms, lets out a laugh. The more
DAVID laughs the more KING does it.
DAVID joins in as Mariah. They fall on top of
each other and laugh. A while passes.*

DAVID   All that time imagining and I couldn't even
get it up. And there I was spoutin what
marriage was and what it wasn't. Yet here
I am in some hotel room with all your
superhero cum across my chest and I have to
admit... I like it.

KING   You imagined us?

DAVID   (*Quickly deflecting.*) Syd'll say I'm fallin
back into bad habits.

KING   (*Stretching his arms yawning, coyly.*) I'm a bad
habit, am I?

DAVID .   Will you tell Raheem?

KING   If he asks I won't lie.

                  KING *sits up.*

DAVID   Do you remember when we met?

KING   Raheem's birthday.

DAVID   Correct. But we didn't talk that night.

KING   Didn't we?

DAVID   No... I saw you on the Tube the next day and
             was like, that's the guy, the American guy from
             the party. You were readin a book. *Pinter Plays
             Three*. Your finger, it was underscorin each line
             like the words might disappear.

KING   That wasn't me.

DAVID   Well, it was, so there.

             KING *now scrolling through his phone as*
             DAVID *takes in the room.*

             Who is it?

KING   The Argentinian bear from the pub last night.
             He wants me to go to his club night.

             *He removes a pubic hair from his tongue and
             holds it up to the light.*

             I can always tell when they're Stevie's.

             *They both stare at it as though it were an
             exhibit in a gallery.*

DAVID   He's mine.

KING   How can you tell?

DAVID   Yours are curlier.

KING   (*Teasingly.*) Get you, Wagatha Christie.

DAVID   Could always be Don's.

             KING *playfully climbs on top of* DAVID *and
             tries to put the pubic hair in his face. They
             play-fight like a couple of kids,* DAVID
             *screaming for him to stop, recoiling, but
             enjoying.*

No. No. Get off. Get off!

KING *pins him down. The music stops. He kisses him, then notices the scars on* DAVID's *arm.*

They're old.

KING *traces the scars as if drawing them.* DAVID, *now vulnerable, pulls away. He covers his arm.* KING *backs off into the shadows to find his clothes.* DAVID *puts on his T-shirt and trousers.*

How ya gettin home? I suppose you could walk. It's nice out… Did I tell you my therapist looks like Tilda Swinton in *The Beach*. She has all these –

KING *has become* CRAW.

CRAW	You're a good man in a bad world.
DAVID	Y'wha?
CRAW	Sometimes it's hard for a good man to be king.

CRAW *steps out of the shadows, hovering above* DAVID.

DAVID	Oh… my… *God*.
CRAW	(*Edging towards* DAVID.) The forces of darkness, they're sent to try us.

CRAW *postures, his chest expanding as he morphs into* DAVID's *fantasy. Even his breathing has changed.* CRAW *grunts something inaudible.*

DAVID	What is it? What's wrong?
CRAW	Must return.
DAVID	Stay!
CRAW	I –

DAVID   (*Now begging*.) Stay, please.

               CRAW *grabs* DAVID *into a lock*. DAVID,
               held and protected, frantically kisses CRAW's
               arms.

               My king, my monarch.

CRAW   Can't.

DAVID   Come back to bed.

CRAW   (*Trying to bat him off but failing*.) Let go.

DAVID   Okay… But if I let go can I sit on yer face?

               DAVID, *having got what he wanted, now lets
               go. He sits up in the bed*. CRAW *turns and
               leans in touching between* DAVID's *legs*.
               DAVID *lets out a moan*.

CRAW   You like that, huh?

DAVID   Yes! I fuckin *love* that. (*Whispering*.) Breed
               me!

CRAW   I have a queen.

DAVID   Get yaself a new one.

CRAW   I have a queen back in Crawtopia.

DAVID   (*Fervently, almost pleading*.) She don't
               deserve you!

CRAW   But you're a mortal.

DAVID   And you're a fuckin god! Breed me!

CRAW   (*With torment*.) I'm a symbol of something.
               I can't lie.

               DAVID *clutching at him*.

DAVID   Craw never lies. When they go low

CRAW   We go high

DAVID   When they go low

CRAW	We go
DAVID	(*Flustered.*) Oh God!
	DAVID *cries out in ecstasy as* CRAW *pushes him away and looks down at him.*
CRAW	(*With utter sincerity.*) We'll do this again one day.
DAVID	When?
CRAW	I don't know. One day when my life isn't imploding.
DAVID	Cool.
	Smoke appears. A glaring bright light. As CRAW, *but also possibly as* KING –
CRAW	David, I do love you, you know that, right?
	CRAW *leans forward, slowly kisses* DAVID, *then makes to go.*
DAVID	Wait! Let me look at you. Let me look at you just like that.
	CRAW *turns.* DAVID *looks at him just like that.*
	Okay… You can go.
	CRAW *holds up his hand in a salute and calls out –*
CRAW	Crawtopia in Excelsis!
	DAVID *returning the salute.*
DAVID	(*Breathlessly.*) Crawtopia in Excelsis!
	A low rumble shakes the entire theatre. CRAW *vanishes.*

Scene Five

SYD	He's married, ya dozy melt.
DAVID	I know that.
SYD	Pass.

He passes her the costume.

	Was he hung?
DAVID	Leave it out.
SYD	Well, how big we talkin?

He hesitates to answer. Then –

DAVID	It was pleasant.
SYD	Bwoi. They used to say that in GCSE caterin about my apple strudel. So what, you think he'll chuck in the travel writer, ask you to marry him?
DAVID	(*Incredulously.*) You reckon?
SYD	Judith Chalmers ain't gonna put up with tha shit for long, I can tell ya.

A child screams violently from off.

	Stickin it to a married man never ends well. No one wants to be Camilla.
DAVID	Camilla played the long game and ended up the winner. Certainly alive, at least!
SYD	If someone emotionally available came along you wouldn't know what to do.

He doesn't reply.

	How was yer therapy?
DAVID	Yeah, it's goin good, y'know. Every time I go I feel like I'm in a Woody Allen movie.
SYD	That a good thing?

SYD *looks out to the garden.*

You clock that dad?

DAVID   Where?

She nods, they look.

SYD   He is a treat. God-tier.

DAVID   We're here to service the kids, not the fathers.

SYD   It's a bespoke service, bro… (*Looking out approvingly.*) I'd definitely bruise my knees for that.

DAVID   Stickin it to a married man… never ends well.

SYD   Oh, don't worry about me, babes. I'm 'appy with my Jake.

DAVID   You sure about that?

SYD   Craw from Crawtopia's clearly poundin everythin in sight. Never mind his superpowers, get down that clap clinic, love, make sure you ain't got an STD. It's poor Stevie I feel sorriest for. You saw what women like Mum put up with.

DAVID   Mum weren't exactly Maria von Trapp.

SYD   Maria von Trapp didn't have to deal with Redbridge Council.

DAVID   I been talkin about it in my therapy.

SYD   What, King?

DAVID   Dad.

SYD   He weren't that bad.

DAVID   You were his princess, you would say that.

SYD   Why you always gotta come wit the bad stuff for? There were good times too.

DAVID   Were there?

SYD	You remember what you want, innit. Easy to think of when he weren't there. What about all the times he was? Chessington.
DAVID	Once. He took us once.
SYD	Once more than a lot of other blokes would.

A beat. She clocks his brand-new Nike Air VaporMax.

Where'd you get them?

DAVID *doesn't answer.*

I'm still waitin on my rent!

DAVID	You'll get yer rent. Chill.
SYD	You spoken to him?
DAVID	To who?
SYD	What ya mean, who? The King of the Swingers. The jungle VIP.
DAVID	Nah. Is what it is, innit.

She gives him side-eye.

SYD	These man-boys.
DAVID	I feel sorry for him.
SYD	Why? Geezer's a wrong'un.
DAVID	But it must be 'ard.
SYD	He likes it 'ard. What you expect, man look like that... I told you, you don't wanna get mixed up in it. Wait and the right person'll come.
DAVID	He ain't though, has he?... Y'know, when I was a teenager I'd see couples, even ugly couples, usually white, and I'd think if I come out that can be me. So I came out, and guess what? No one. No dark knight in shinin armour. Not even someone I'd vaguely let fiddle with me on a regular basis. Went through all my twenties thinkin don't worry,

	he'll come. Well, I'm almost forty now, and he still hasn't, has he?
SYD	Boy just need a man.
DAVID	No! I want fun! Jus cos you wouldn't do it don't mean the rest of us can't.
SYD	Involvin other people in your sex life is a risk.
DAVID	(*With assurance.*) Yeah, but you can mitigate those risks. And… they might. Look at the Bloomsbury Set. Down each other's holes like rabbits. Never did them any harm.
SYD	(*Shaking her head, laughing.*) Open. It's just another word for greedy.
DAVID	Yeah, well, yer a dirty little straight, inch'ya.
SYD	Gays didn't invent open relationships, y'know. This is some Byzantine shit that's been goin on since before the Romans.
DAVID	Maybe it's his second adolescence.
SYD	(*Laughing.*) Second adolescence? Lawd, lawd, lawd.
DAVID	What? Gays don't get one. Not the first time.
SYD	Lots of us don't. Mum, she didn't! Married at sixteen, weren't till thirty she got one either. This shit ain't homo-specific. King's jus havin what us heteros call a midlife crisis… (*Now dressed as a Crawtopian, she stares at him, smiles and shakes her head.*) Gays. Spend a lifetime fightin for what we've got, finally go and get it, then realise all they wanted was what they had to begin with. No marriage and loadsa cock!

DAVID *doesn't reply.*

Listen, yer doin good, bruv. Gotta keep doin good, ya get me? Little exercise each day, go to ya therapy, eat well. Bare minimum.

DAVID	I know.
SYD	I know ya know. (*With a smile.*) Just remindin you, innit.
	Kids party music from off. Maybe S Club 7. SYD *turns to* DAVID.
	I got some news... Jake and I... we're pregnant.
DAVID	Get out.
SYD	Straight up. I took the test this mornin. Yer gunna be an uncle.
DAVID	Uncle David. Oh, I like that. That's got a ring to it, y'know... How ya feelin?
SYD	Scared. Excited... It's what we wanted so I'm happy... I gotta wait so don't tell a livin soul.
DAVID	Don't fuck it up, yeah?
SYD	We'll try not to. (*As she goes.*) Let's crack on.
	She leaves. DAVID *stares down at his superhero costume.* KING *appears. The music cuts out.*

Scene Six

DAVID	Yer soaked.
KING	I been walkin the streets for the last hour. Stevie threw me out. I didn't even have time to change. My car keys – they were in the house.
DAVID	Can I get you anythin? Cuppa tea?
KING	Would you mind if I stay?
DAVID	Course!
KING	Only if you're sure. I don't wanna be no bother.
DAVID	You ain't.
KING	We were meant to be at a friend's birthday.
DAVID	What 'appened?
KING	He went through my Twitter account and found my alt.
DAVID	You have an alt?
KING	I don't post anythin. He's over-reactin.
DAVID	Hold on a sec. Rewind.
KING	This guy and I were DMing each other. He sent me a picture of his hole.
DAVID	His hole?
KING	Yes. His hole.
DAVID	You mean like his actual hole?
KING	Yes. His actual hole. I know it was silly. But – it's just fantasy. Everyone does it.
DAVID	(*Trying to suppress his judgement.*) They do?
	A beat.
KING	Mind if I take a shower?
DAVID	I'll fetch a towel.

	DAVID goes off. KING's *phone rings, he answers.*
KING	What? None of your business. Cos you behave like a psycho. This is boring. I didn't say you're boring, I said *it's* boring…
	He kisses his teeth. DAVID *returns, holding a towel.*
	Well, either you get on board or…
	STEVEN *has hung up.*
	Stevie? Stevie?!
DAVID	(*Handing him the towel.*) …Is he okay? With us, I mean.
KING	I suppose he's always been suspicious.
DAVID	Of me?
KING	More of Raheem. I told him we shared a bed, he thought it was cute. Where's Syd?
DAVID	Out with the fetus.
	KING *sits on the floor. He sees* DAVID's *copy of* Hamlet *and picks it up.*
KING	Want me to test you?
DAVID	Oh, I weren't gonna learn it. Why? You'd learn it wouldn't you?
KING	Depends.
	He stares at DAVID.
	Do you want it?
DAVID	Ain't fussed.
KING	(*Bashfully, making to get up.*) I should go.
DAVID	(*Immediately.*) Stay.
	He pushes KING *to the floor and sits on his lap.*

I been asked to prepare a song. They're
openin the show with a Negro spiritual.

An all-black production directed by a white
woman in which we all sing Negro spirituals.

KING   Maybe they're bein ironic.

DAVID scrunches up his face. KING *goes
back to the earmarked page.*

And what if it tempt you toward the flood,
my lord...

DAVID   Or to the dreadful summit of the cliff –
That beetles o'er his base into the sea –

And there... (*A little stuck.*) there... assume
some other horrible form which...

KING   Which might deprive...

DAVID   Which might deprive your sovereignty of
reason –
And draw you into...

KING   Madness.

DAVID   Madness.

They kiss. KING *stares at him.*

KING   ...So... You think you want it?

DAVID   I...

DAVID *suddenly gets up.*

KING   Then fuck it. Fuck it all off.

DAVID   Tha's alright for you to say, I gotta pay rent.

KING   I can help.

Pause.

I was thinkin. How would you feel about
joining me at the end of the press tour in
Australia? Change of scenery. Flights all
taken care of.

DAVID   I can't.

KING   Why not? You ever been? You'd *love* it!
           (*Genuinely.*) Don't answer now, have a think.
           Might be fun. Who knows, you might even
           enjoy it.

           *DAVID stares. KING's whole chest has
           expanded. DAVID is cock-struck, KING
           gets up.*

           Right. I need to shower. I kinda reek.

           *He makes to go, DAVID watches him. He
           suddenly turns.*

           Oh, if Stevie messages you, don't tell him I'm
           here.

           *KING exits. DAVID waits. He puts on the
           trainers. As he does a loud bell rings out.*

Scene Seven

STEVEN   David!

           DAVID turns.

           I thought it was you.

DAVID   Stevie... Hi! Oh my God.

STEVEN   Hi.

           *STEVEN clutches a theatre programme as
           they embrace. The bell stops.*

           Alright?

DAVID   Good, ta, yeah. You?

STEVEN   Yeah. You well?

DAVID   Yeah, *really* well.

STEVEN   Good, good.

STEVEN *touches* DAVID*'s arm.*

Are you watching?

DAVID   Yeah.

STEVEN   Me too. I'm with my publisher. She's over there. I think she's gonna drop me.

He laughs nervously. They look over to her. A brief moment of apprehension.

You look well.

DAVID   Do I?

STEVEN   Yeah. Yeah, you look really well. Like the trainers. King's got those. Wears them when he's trying to be trendy.

He smiles at DAVID.

I heard about your night together. Sounds like you had fun.

DAVID   Sorry?

STEVEN *touches* DAVID*'s arm again.*

STEVEN   For what? It's fine. I'd soon say if it wasn't. Besides, it's what we agreed. As long as it stays private whoever he and I... y'know. Strictly *entre nous*, between us girls. But, like I say, he should make the most of it. Seize the moment so to speak. He's not gonna be this physically attractive forever. Crawtopia will only last so long. I keep telling him. Men of that age are often taken by – well – pretty things. A sensible husband shrugs and laughs.

DAVID   So last month?

STEVEN   Oh, that? That was just me being silly. Sometimes I talk like I don't know what. I get jealous. But, well, our counsellor said, oh what did she say. She said relationships aren't about who you are – or who you were when

you met – but how you evolve. It's important
I afford King this room to change. To not
define him by his current limitations, cos that
would just put him in a box which may not
allow space for a better more fully realised
version of himself to take root.

A beat.

I'm sure we can work our way through it. But
anyway, you mustn't feel any sort of – I mean,
there's no oddness. Not from me.

STEVEN *looks at* DAVID *almost bashfully.*

In a way I have to admit, I found it rather hot.

DAVID   You did?

STEVEN   Yes! Part of me wished I'd been there
             watching.

             DAVID *uncertain how to respond.*

             Three in a bed. Me sandwiched between two
             hot black men. We should try it.

DAVID   I ain't ever had a threesome.

STEVEN   It was a joke, Dave.

             DAVID *falls silent.*

             Have you seen this play before?

DAVID   No... I hear it's long.

STEVEN   King warned me it might be before he flew off
             to LA this morning. Didn't he say? I thought
             he'd mention.

             DAVID *unable to hide his surprise.*

             He said you had an audition or ...

DAVID   Yeah, didn't hear back.

             STEVEN *pulls a sad face.*

             Oh, I didn't want it anyway.

STEVEN   Right... You know he's obsessed with this guy. Don. I'm talking *obsessed*. He writes King songs and sends them as voicenotes. I've heard them, they're terrible. Don said they can't be together, but King's lost his mind all the same.

The bell rings out again, followed by an announcement.

TANNOY   (*Voice-over.*) This evening's performance will commence in one minute. You have one minute. Thank you.

STEVEN   Will you go out and see him on the press tour do you think?

DAVID   Probably not. No... You?

STEVEN   He asked if I wanna go out for Cannes but I have a deadline coming up. Wine tasters are gagging for my opinion of the Côte-d'Or, apparently.

He makes to leave, then suddenly stops.

You know, some nights we bicker, fight. Go to bed angry, usually over stupid stuff that doesn't matter but somehow absolutely does in that moment. But we like being married. The one thing that seems clear is that we love each other. Deeply.

The bell rings. STEVEN smiles weakly, quickly gathers himself and makes to go.

Will you be sticking around after?

DAVID   Yeah.

STEVEN   Great. I'll see you on the other side. Bye.

DAVID   Bye.

STEVEN leaves. DAVID suddenly struggles for breath.

Scene Eight

They regain their breath as they stretch.

RAHEEM	Open marriage may be the best thing that's ever happened to him. He's even started dressin different, you noticed?

DAVID *pulls his legs back.*

You gunna go?

DAVID	You're tellin me you wouldn't?

DAVID *doing the downward dog.*

RAHEEM	Funny. I thought the King only likes white dick, to play in the snow.
DAVID	If he only likes white dick why'd he sleep with me?
RAHEEM	Four bottles of prosecco plus the mandy we took in the toilet, I should imagine.
DAVID	You took drugs that night?
RAHEEM	Ah – bredrin, come. Just cos you don't no more don't mean the rest of us can't.

They stretch. After a while DAVID *takes in* RAHEEM*'s ripped body.*

DAVID	We did it again. Last week. The King and I, we slept together again.
RAHEEM	Verify slept.
DAVID	Stevie threw him out. One thing led to another, we flip-fucked.

RAHEEM *stares.*

There were sustained multiple orgasms.

RAHEEM	Oh, Hermione. Ten points to Gryffindor. (*Laughing.*) SO YA FUCKING CRAW?!
DAVID	Keep ya voice down!

RAHEEM	God save the King, eh?
	RAHEEM *lays on his back, pulls his legs into his body and hugs himself.*
	Well, now ya gotta go, innit.
	A beat.
	You told Syd?
DAVID	Course.
RAHEEM	What she say?
	Snap to SYD –
SYD	FUCKIN AUSTRALIA?
DAVID	Stop shoutin!
SYD	Ya know what happened to Susan's brother!
DAVID	Oh my God Susan's brother.
SYD	(*The words tumble out of her.*) *He* had a breakdown, went travellin to Australia, got knifed by a racist Uber driver who hated black people. That what you want? You wanna get yerself stabbed up Down Under by some racist Uber driver?
DAVID	I can't talk when ya like this.
SYD	If he cares so much where was he last year, aye? Nah, where was he? And another thing, I know you've been missin yer therapy!
DAVID	How?
SYD	You come home too happy!
DAVID	I ain't gotta explain meself.
SYD	When'd you last go?
DAVID	Yesterday.
SYD	Lies! Ain't nothin casual about casual sex with a mate, Dave, nothin, ya get me?

DAVID	Might be good. Change of scenery. Might be nice.
SYD	Noshin off Idris Elba might be nice. Don't you think we all might wanna run away? That's the easy route, bruv, bad dumb-arse choices'll stop you from havin to really look at yaself.
DAVID	I do look at meself. I look at meself every day and I'm tired.
SYD	Doin the work *is* tirin, don't mean don't do it!

DAVID *looks away.*

If you go it'll jus keep you in this place where you're hoping, prayin, wishin against hope, with irrational hope, that if King hammers away at you for long enough, and if he keeps his superhero dick in your arse for long enough he'll somehow fall in love with you.

Snap back to –

DAVID	She was happy for me.
RAHEEM	(*Instructing* DAVID.) Keep goin.

DAVID *applies pressure to* RAHEEM*'s body as he stretches.*

Does Stevie know?

DAVID	He suggested a threesome.
RAHEEM	Oh my God. A thirsty little throuple.
DAVID	I never thought Stevie liked us. You've seen how defensive he gets.

Snap to STEVEN *and* KING –

STEVEN	I don't want to centre myself here by doing that classic white-person thing, but in a way I found it slightly aggressive.
DAVID	All the white people in the audience were asked to get up on stage, he goes –

STEVEN	I totally get the play's thesis, it just felt a little… I dunno.
DAVID	A play about white appropriation and *he* feels attacked.
KING	Well, let's unpack that.
STEVEN	I mean, I get the whole white-gaze thing, but –
DAVID	A fuckin travel writer from Ealing.
STEVEN	If anything it just pointed out how many white people go to the theatre.
KING	Isn't that a comment in its own way, babe?
DAVID	(*With contempt.*) Babe.
	DAVID *pushes harder against* RAHEEM.
STEVEN	My vision of the world is expanded each day by standing at your side.
RAHEEM	He said that?
DAVID	He *actually* said that.
STEVEN	Not all white liberals are the enemy.
DAVID	White middle-class liberals are the ugly of the world.
STEVEN	I mean, some might argue they're the ones bankrolling theatres to begin with.
DAVID	Y'know Stevie's dad supported Section 28.
STEVEN	I'm just saying now's not the time for wistful sentimentality.
DAVID	Didn't go to their weddin.
STEVEN	It's time for action!
DAVID	When we go Black Pride Stevie goes Babington House!
STEVEN	I mean, I'd love a black play that's not about race, that's about, I dunno. Jazz?

DAVID	*Then* the billion-dollar white-liberal mic drop.
STEVEN	I know more about racism than most white people.
DAVID	And so I explain that the white people invited up on to that stage have invariably never been seen as white like that in their entire lives, even when in Africa or wherever.
STEVEN	I felt *very* white when I visited the Congo, actually.
DAVID	(*As he presses aggressively against* RAHEEM.) HE'S A FUCKIN WASTEMAN!!!
RAHEEM	David!
DAVID	HE LIKES MUMFORD AND SONS / FOR FUCK'S SAKE!
RAHEEM	OW! OW! OW!
	STEVEN *disappears*. DAVID *leans off*. *A while passes*. DAVID *sits motionless*.
DAVID	When I can't sleep I watch the Craw films.
RAHEEM	Me too.
DAVID	Always the Craw films.
RAHEEM	Me too.
DAVID	Okay. But I mean specifically the one where Craw's bein chased by Sellapath and the streets are besieged by giant flames.
RAHEEM	(*With admiration*.) *Craw and the Stolen Army*.
DAVID	Craw appears in an alley in a beam of light all noble n hot and godlike n shit.
	CRAW *appears in an alley in a beam of light all noble and hot and godlike and shit*.
RAHEEM	The one with Zendaya.

DAVID	She's starin down at him from the clock tower.
	ZENDAYA *descends*.
	She got tha whole Nubian earth-mother vibe-type ting goin on.
RAHEEM	Goddess.
DAVID	She reveals Craw is in actual fact her son and was conceived in the days before Crawtopia came into existence, and is now the Craw's duty –
RAHEEM	Nay, his birthright
DAVID	Okay, it's his birthright to save the planet from extremist right-wing propaganda… Zendaya's eyeballin him.
	CRAW *deep bows to* ZENDAYA.
RAHEEM	*So* hot.
DAVID	*So* hot. I mean you wouldn't wanna mess with this bitch.
RAHEEM	I did her for Halloween last year.
DAVID	…She places her hand on Craw's shoulder and says –
ZENDAYA	(*In a worthy black earth-mother American accent.*) Second by millisecond by nanosecond the universe shudders and expands. In every quadrant.
	DAVID *and* RAHEEM *perhaps mouth her words to themselves.*
	In every dimension the forces of evil keep pace with those of good. Where will you stand, my chil'? On which side will your allegiances lie? Only God knows.
DAVID	Then the evil Sellapath comes n tries to take away all Craw's power.

	STEVEN *appears as* SELLAPATH. *He's hideous. He tries to take away all* CRAW's *power.*
RAHEEM	He falls to his knees and temporarily dies.
	CRAW *dies.* ZENDAYA *and* SELLAPATH *disappear.*
DAVID	Till the next instalment.
RAHEEM	(*With longing.*) *Craw Control.*
DAVID	King can turn even the worst of films into a better one.
RAHEEM	True dat.
DAVID	S'why people like him.
RAHEEM	For real.
DAVID	(*Caught in emotion.*) S'why I…
RAHEEM	Yeah.
	Pause. DAVID *looks at* RAHEEM *stretching, all muscly and beefcaked up.*
DAVID	He's fucked him. He's fucked him I can tell
	ZENDAYA *and* SELLAPATH *reappear out of the darkness.*
ZENDAYA	Hush, chil'
SELLAPATH	But why would he tell you to journey to the promised land?
DAVID	The wha?
ZENDAYA	Down Under, David. Down Under.
DAVID	He wants me to think he's above it all.
SELLAPATH	Like Jada Pinkett Smith at her red table?
DAVID	Yes!! Like Jada Pinkett Smith at her red table.
SELLAPATH	Why do you care if your friends sleep with each other, bro?

DAVID	Cos I don't like em havin more sex than me.
ZENDAYA	(*As both* SYD *and* ZENDAYA.) That's basically all of them.
SELLAPATH	You could always ask
DAVID	But then he might tell me the truth
ZENDAYA	The truth being?
DAVID	King fingered Raheem at Stevie Wonder in Hyde Park.
ZENDAYA	And the Craw told you this?
DAVID	No, other people, other people told me.
SELLAPATH	So you don't actually know –
DAVID	(*Swinging round facing* RAHEEM.) You mind if I ask you somethin?
RAHEEM	(*Looking up from the ground, still stretching.*) Yes, I'll be your maid of honour.
	DAVID *stares down hard at* RAHEEM*'s perfect body and takes a deep breath.*
DAVID	You and King, have you ever…
RAHEEM	What?
DAVID	Slept together. Have you slept together?
RAHEEM	Have we slept together?
DAVID	(*To the superheroes.*) He just kept repeatin.
RAHEEM	Have we slept together?
DAVID	It was kinda like he enjoyed…
RAHEEM	Have we slept together?
DAVID	Yeah. Have you slept together?
RAHEEM	Have we?
DAVID	Yes

RAHEEM *mulls it over.*

RAHEEM   No.

          A beat.

          But he did finger me at Stevie Wonder in
          Hyde Park.

DAVID   I don't fuckin believe this

RAHEEM   Sometimes we say things to each other

DAVID   Said they say things to each other

RAHEEM   Like stuff we'd like to do

DAVID   Now all I think of is stuff they'd like to do

RAHEEM   We've this weird kinda 'you're mine, but not
          mine' ting, ya get me? Perhaps in another life.
          But he is *not* mine, David. And I, I am most
          certainly not his... Come, we go.

          RAHEEM *runs off.* DAVID *watches.*
          ZENDAYA *and* SELLAPATH *fly out.*

DAVID   I told my therapist I was 'avin trouble sleepin.

          She said what is it you dream about.

          I couldn't answer. She told me to keep a diary.

          Like a diary of my dreams.

          Something like 'My Other Voice' by Sparks
          emanates around the space.

          I begin to notice. I notice the thing I dream of is
          the exact same thing I dreamed of as a child:
          bein rescued. Not by just anyone, but
          specifically by a superhero... Next session I tell
          her this she says but who is this superhero,
          David, what does he look like?

          I tell her once he's rescued me he'd then fuck
          me, truck me, make me his... So in a sense it
          was like...

He can't say it.

Only I lie. I lie and tell her the superhero is just some generic white Chris Pratt prototype kinda shit, and she looks at me with this awful crushin pity as if to say God bless this little mixed-up faggot in need of a white saviour, and so this, *this* is what I let her believe, that I'm some homo cliché A-grade freak, which I undoubtedly am.

CRAW *suddenly emerges, a dark, saintly figure.*

She says little boys need their fathers. But little black boys need their fathers more.

A beat.

He wouldn't have invited me if he didn't need me, that's what I keep tellin myself. That maybe he does. He needs me. He needs me. He does. He needs me.

As the music grows louder we see CRAW standing above him in the shadow. DAVID, no longer able to fight it, turns and looks up.

Blackout.

Interval.

ACT TWO

Scene One

Something like Jeff Buckley 'Be Your Husband'. It ends. DAVID whistles in astonishment.

DAVID   (*In amazement.*) Rah! Everythin's so clean. So white, so clean.

             KING *takes* DAVID*'s suitcase. An attractive* ROOM SERVICE *guy enters holding a dirty cup.*

KING   (*To* ROOM SERVICE.) We're good.

             ROOM SERVICE *smiles, exits.*

DAVID   (*Quietly, referring to* ROOM SERVICE*'s attractiveness.*) Oh. My. God.

KING   Not my type.

             KING *puts down the suitcase, they kiss.*

             You look beautiful. (*Holding him.*) Oh. One of the producers invited us to dinner.

DAVID   Us? Sounds official.

KING   He's in the middle of a crisis. A kid accused him of inappropriate behaviour. (*From* DAVID*'s look.*) Kid as in twink, not kid as in a minor! Kwe's a lotta things, but he's not that. This kid says he used to call Kwe Daddy Crawtopia. Says Kwe paid him for sex in coke. But everyone knew it was an affair. Even Kwe's wife.

             A knock on the door. KING *calls out.*

             Come in!

JACKSON *enters. White, boyish, Aussie and well-groomed.*

JACKSON   'Lo.

KING   Jackson, this is David.

JACKSON   Hey. (*Immediately to* KING.) So, Production sent an email. They want you to consider, not consider, reconsider how you'll talk about working with Kwe.

KING   Why? Did I say something wrong?

JACKSON   No, no, not at all. But after New York they're worried there might be questions. There's a strategy briefing tomorrow, this is just a heads-up. I booked your table for eight.

KING   Great. (*His phone rings, he looks.*) Stevie. One sec. (*He answers.*) Yo!

He leaves. A moment. We hear KING, *his words inaudible, from off.* JACKSON *looks at* DAVID.

JACKSON   (*With a smile.*) Cool trainers… You must be King's friend, right?

DAVID   (*Politely.*) Yeah.

JACKSON   Where you from?

DAVID   London.

JACKSON   Fantastic. Which part?

DAVID   Brixton

JACKSON   Cool. Yer parents?

DAVID   Brixton.

JACKSON   And their parents?… Jokes. I dated a black guy. He got it all the time.

KING   (*From off.*) But why, why can't we all be together and just have a nice time?

DAVID *looks to* JACKSON *who smiles.*
KING*'s conversation trails off.*

JACKSON   (*In a cod whisper.*) They had a little fight. The
            husband, he's flying out. You ever get high?

DAVID   Pardon?

JACKSON   Drugs, do you do drugs?

DAVID   No.

JACKSON   …Well… Sounds like you're gonna have
            a fantastic trip.

            KING *re-enters.*

KING   Sorry. Stevie maintenance.

JACKSON   You need anythin else?

KING   (*Looking up.*) Er, yeah… There was a
            problem with the light.

JACKSON   I'll have concierge send someone up. Aria,
            eight o'clock. See you then.

            JACKSON *goes. A beat.*

DAVID   (*Smiling through his upset.*) He's comin?

KING   He's a nice kid.

DAVID   I meant Stevie.

KING   I didn't know myself until this morning. He's
            taken a Bolt to Heathrow. He sounds drunk…
            (*As if he might cry.*) Sorry. You don't need
            this. I'm such an ass.

DAVID   It's fine.

KING   Look, tomorrow after my morning junket we'll
            all go to the beach. Coogee. Wylie's. The
            Botanic Gardens. We can soak up the sun.

DAVID   Why am I startin to feel like one of the wives
            of a leader of a cult?

KING	That's kinda hot.
	They kiss.
	Elder David.
DAVID	You could buy us all a commune. We could live like Mormons.
	They kiss again.
KING	We'll have fun. I promise... Craw never lies, remember?
	He smiles, picks up DAVID*'s suitcase and goes off to the bedroom.*
	Come!
	DAVID *smiles. He follows.*

Scene Two

KWEKU *sits there. Black, American, bisexual, slightly older than everyone else. He is mid-conversation. As the meal concludes, they all drink wine, apart from* DAVID.

KWEKU	(*He sniffs.*) I don't think you need to be a dog to direct *Lassie*.
KING	(*With enthusiasm.*) David's an activist.
JACKSON	Can I try?
	KING *feeds* JACKSON *his sushi.* DAVID *watches.*
KWEKU	The director is black.
DAVID	He's straight!
KWEKU	So what, you think you have to be it to make it. Is that what you're saying?
DAVID	I believe representation matters.

KWEKU	But at expense of the art?
JACKSON	(*Of the food*.) This is *sooo* good.
DAVID	Isn't that what people frightened of representation say?
KWEKU	I'm not sure I subscribe to this weird notion that ideology is the art.
JACKSON	My brother's straight, he cried. Though he also cried during *Thor: Ragnarok*.
KWEKU	To see a story like that prosper the same year when all we were seeing was young black body after black body taken from us. (*Sniffs*.) I stopped watching CBS.
JACKSON	Mahershala Ali gives my heart a boner.
KWEKU	There's an insecurity surrounding black hyper-masculinity, I see it in the kids my children go to school with. All this is entrenched. Where had we seen that kind of story?
KING	(*Taking out his card*.) This is on me.
KWEKU	No, no, no, put that away. I won't hear of it.
	KWEKU *takes out his wallet.*
	So, David. If you hated a bona fide black masterpiece, what exactly do you like?
KING	(*Light-heartedly*.) We'll be here all night.
DAVID	I didn't say I hated it. I just thought they left out all the joy.
	JACKSON *looks at* KING *who is looking at* KWEKU *who is looking at* DAVID.
KING	Do you have any coke?
JACKSON	I'll WhatsApp my dealer. (*Messaging his dealer*.) He lives in the next street.
DAVID	Gays tend to praise work representin us for the fact it represents us at all, they rarely care for the quality of that representation. I mean,

sure, lots of gays and straight women might agree it's a masterpiece, but it's like, I occupy this world, I wake up in it. They leave stuff out! They ignore the very essence of what it is to be alive and repackage my culture and sell it to me as some dirge underscored by an oboe? The most valiant drug dealer in the history of cinema? Of course whites love it, it's a neoliberal's wet dream. A lacklustre handjob on a beach? Please. How can ya make a gay film wid *no* gay sex?

KWEKU *sniffs*. KING *does the universal sign for the bill*.

KWEKU   (*Laughing*.) I'm sorry, why do you keep sayin gay sex? (*Sniffs*.) Isn't it just... sex?

DAVID   I look up porn online, I type gay sex, cos sex n gay sex are two different things.

KWEKU   Are they?

JACKSON   Oh, they are.

KING   If we wanna make the club we should head.

DAVID   Not showin gay sex gives a big free pass to all the squeamish straights who reject that part of our lives. A story about gay black male desire? Like, is that *all* the gay sex they can have? Are you seriously tellin me he wouldn't have fucked that guy a million ways till Sunday at the end? It was implausible. It was post-queer. I've seen versions of this story my whole life, the black victim overwhelmed by the system. Even *The Color Purple* had a few laughs, for fuck's sake! Queers ARE funny!

JACKSON   (*A little drunk*.) Print that on a T-shirt.

DAVID   WE ARE! Society had no place for us, we had to be. It's possible to portray us as fun and sensitive, the two aren't mutually exclusive yet all I saw was victim victim victim, this endless parade of shame, and it's like, okay you know, after being born black *and* gay in a straight white world humour *is*, it's king and quite possibly the only defence we have. Cos I'm tellin you if things were only ever *that* bleak, like, if there was no light, not a smidgen of hope, I would've killed myself a long time ago.

An unbearable silence. All eyes now on DAVID. KWEKU *sniffs, wipes his nose and smiles.*

KING   I think the waiters are waiting for us to go.

JACKSON   (*Getting up.*) My dealer.

KING   I'll come too. I suddenly feel like I need some air. (*He glances at* DAVID.)

They go.

KWEKU   (*Staring at* DAVID.) Well, this has been a delight... Press weeks are usually full of people with very intense friendliness and nothing behind the eyes. You're the only person on this trip I've found remotely interesting.

He sniffs.

King says you're an actor. Perhaps I've seen you in somethin?

DAVID   I'm not masculine or handsome enough to warrant the kind of attention King gets.

KWEKU   You don't drink? Is there a reason?

DAVID   Why's there gotta be a reason?

KWEKU   Just askin.

DAVID says nothing.

You an only child?

DAVID   Sister. I got a sister.

KWEKU   Is she as dour as you?

Again DAVID *doesn't reply.*

So, why you think you're not masculine enough, huh?

DAVID   …A lotta black guys 'ave this thing. Gotta work 'ard. Gotta work 'arder than everyone else. Gotta be good, gotta be twice as good. We're sold it by our fathers.

KWEKU   Ambition?

DAVID   Discipline. The same discipline that gets you a tight ripped body or arms the size of horses' withers. Maybe if I had it no one might notice my legion of personality flaws.

KWEKU   And there was me thinking you didn't like victims.

They hold each other's gaze. KWEKU *looks at him as if studying a piece of merchandise.*

Dude, who the fuck hurt you?

DAVID *doesn't reply.*

Y'know what I think? I think we're not in control. Every now and then something happens to reiterate that fact, to stop our personal growth. Some cave at the thought. They spend a life tryna escape all they know about themselves, usually through meaningless goals or achievements – (*Sniffs.*) things we know to be shallow. Or things like religion or art. Anything we can say is significant in a life that ultimately is not. But we are *not* in control. If we were we'd know far better than to give a shit about anythin.

KWEKU *picks up his wine and drinks. He looks at* DAVID.

What's your American accent like?

Scene Three

DAVID	He must think I fell off the back of the Christmas tree yesterday.
KING	For all you know this could be an opportunity. He was being nice!
DAVID	He was bein a creep! He really thinks that whole blaxploitation pimp act works?
KING	(*On the phone.*) Hi. Yeah. The light in my room, somethin's wrong with it. Thanks.
DAVID	It's true what they say. Power corrupts. And absolute power corrupts arseholes.
KING	(*Taking off his shirt.*) Well, you spent an awful lot of time talkin to him about open relationships.
DAVID	I was makin conversation.
KING	By remindin me every five seconds of my husband's existence?
DAVID	We were havin a debate.
KING	(*With a laugh.*) No, *you* were having a *debate*, *we* were tryna have a nice time.
DAVID	What you sayin? You sayin I embarrassed you, or –
KING	I'm saying you were being a little argumentative.
DAVID	Are we okay?
	KING, *bare-chested, pours more wine and picks up his cigarettes.*
KING	(*In total calmness.*) You wanna know what I think? I think sometimes you need to learn to not be so superior to those who don't believe in the same things you do.
DAVID	Kwe didn't need my permission to talk.

KING	He was being polite. He was! Only you always see red. You're like a dog with a bone.
DAVID	(*Laughing to cover his hurt.*) If that's what you felt then maybe you should've said! Only you *never* say / you just go silent. You don't like confrontation. You rarely say what you feel.
KING	(*Over* DAVID'*s above dialogue at various points.*) David… David… David… (*After* DAVID *says 'feel'.*) Because of this!! Because no one can ever get a fuckin word in!!

KING *indicates to the space in front of him, the space occupied by* DAVID.

I'm sorry Stevie's comin, okay, but don't – don't mock me.

DAVID	Mock you?
KING	Arms the size of horses' withers? Kwe told me in the club. What else you say, ha?
DAVID	Nothin. I say nothin.
KING	Right.
DAVID	You regret askin me 'ere?
KING	(*Calmly.*) Go to bed.

DAVID *lets out a laugh and shakes his head.*

DAVID	You've fucked him.
KING	(*Lighting a cigarette.*) What are you talkin about?
DAVID	That little PR bitch, you've fucked him. I shoulda guessed.
KING	I've not fucked Jackson, David, Jesus!
DAVID	No? He was all over you in that club like white on rice.

KING   Why are we even havin this / conversation?

DAVID   You ask me here, tell me I'm beautiful, say
             come meet my friends, you spend the night
             takin gak in the toilet ignorin me, you know,
             you know I can't be around that shit.

KING   (*With a groan.*) Nobody forced you –

DAVID   I can't be around it! Second adolescence?
             I told Syd, she laughed.

KING   I really don't give two fucks what your sister
             thinks of my marriage. Go to bed.

DAVID   But I wanna talk!

KING   TALK? ALL YOU'VE DONE TONIGHT IS
             FUCKING TALK! I'M SICK OF TALKING!

             Tomorrow I've fifteen fuckin hours of it!
             Strangers asking questions about my private
             life, things they can't ask hidden behind all
             the things they can. (*Edging towards* DAVID,
             *his chest puffing up the more enraged he
             gets*.) I'm over-explainin myself. I had this all
             out yesterday with my therapist and wish
             I never even opened my fuckin mouth. Cos
             straight people can only see marriage from
             how they see it. Everything meaningful to
             them is kids. So if your life ain't built around
             rearin them or your relationships aren't, their
             heads spin. And it's like, fuck that shit! As
             long as you and I both understand what we're
             doin here nobody gets hurt.

             It seems like he might become CRAW.

             You think I'm some kinda schmuck? Don't
             get it twisted, cos I was *always* upfront
             witchu, *always*.

             He goes to him.

             C'mon – c'mon. Don't.

DAVID   I embarrassed you... Syd was right. I should
          never 'ave come.

KING   No, that's not –

DAVID   I wanted to come 'ere and for it all to be
          perfect... but I fuck things up, ya know. I get
          overwhelmed, and so I talk. I talk, I talk, I talk
          and –

KING   C'mon. Shh. Shh. It's okay. Shhh. I'm happy.
          I'm happy you're here.

DAVID   ...Well.

          Pause. Maybe KING *holds* DAVID. *Maybe
          he doesn't.*

          I'm gonna go sleep.

          DAVID *goes to his room.* KING *waits. He
          lights another cigarette. We see* DAVID
          breaking. KING *smokes for a bit. He looks at
          the ring on his finger. He twists it once, stares
          at it for a moment. He stubs out his cigarette
          and goes to approach* DAVID's *bedroom. The
          lights above flicker on and off.* KING *looks
          up. A knock on the door.* KING *calls out.*

KING   Come in!

          He waits. No answer. Another knock.

          I said come in!

          Still no answer. KING *answers it.* ROOM
          SERVICE *stands there.* KING *stares at him.
          A beat.* ROOM SERVICE *enters.* KING *looks
          at him. He walks off.* ROOM SERVICE
          follows.

Scene Four

SYD	Would you care to tell me why I just got the international diallin tone?
DAVID	The signal's bad.
SYD	Your mind's bad! Out here workin my arse off. How bout givin me my rent and the money I laid out for ya phone bill last month, eh?
DAVID	Listen –
SYD	No, you listen, Dave. Ain't no respect. Ain't no courtesy. See why I let you stay? I let you stay cos I care. I let you stay cos I love, bruv.
DAVID	And I'm grateful.
SYD	I'm out 'ere on my tod payin your bills, payin my *own* bills, layin out for my life and yours with a kid on the way, tryna get someone to cover your bookins cos you couldn't be arsed to tell me you weren't gonna show.
DAVID	I don't need no lecture.
SYD	Do you not understand what happened to you? Do you not get if somethin goes wrong again I can't be there this time? I got my own life now. I got my own shit.
DAVID	I know that.
SYD	You seen the photos online?
DAVID	What photos online?
SYD	Oh my days.
DAVID	This is costin coins, sis!

She puts the call on speaker and reads from her phone.

SYD	'Craw heart-throb King Grant has reportedly fallen out with roommate, British travel writer Steven Morris.' (*Kissing her teeth.*) Roommate? Please.

DAVID	You called for this?
SYD	'Photos taken *this weekend* at an exclusive Sydney beach resort show the Craw star strollin arm in arm with his *Fallen Roads* co-star Don Richards without a care in the world. Reps for all parties have declined to comment.' (*Silence.*) …Well. Donald Glover ain't in Atlanta no more, bro. He is not in Atlanta no more!
	A beat.
DAVID	(*To himself.*) …Always the same. Ever since we were kids.
SYD	Come again?
DAVID	Possessive. Controllin.
SYD	What's she chattin about?
DAVID	All the guys you've been with, I never judge, not once!
SYD	You call Jake a fetus!
DAVID	As a joke. I call him it as a joke.
SYD	Well, don't come for me and my man, bruv, we're good, we're tight.
DAVID	If you're havin the geezer's baby I should hope.
SYD	You wanna know why I'm with him?
DAVID	You like young dick?
SYD	I don't give a *fuck* about young dick. I give a fuck whether someone treats me nice. Whether they're respectful. Whether they tell me the truth.
DAVID	Sounds disgustin.
SYD	With all due respect I ain't the one on other side of the planet chasin some grown-arse

fuck-boy who pretends to fly about in latex for a livin.

DAVID   This conversation's reductive.

SYD   Oh, it's reductive, is it, to 'ave someone in your life who gives a toss? Someone who whizzes up the hospital to find the Feds standin by your bed? To collect your shoes still covered in blood from the police? You find that reductive, do you?

DAVID   Know who I ran into the other day? Carla Gardner. You remember Carla? Her mum had a breakdown after the dad left. When we were kids that woman looked like Brigitte Nielsen. Now she has a carer. Carla says her sisters are so possessive she finds it 'ard to breathe. It's the curse of that estate. Fatherless women.

SYD   We weren't fatherless.

DAVID   Disappeared for weeks on end. Came and got us only when he pleased. Left by five at Christmas. He was the baby father.

SYD   Hate that word.

DAVID   You didn't see what I saw.

SYD   My childhood was mine, Dave. Yours was yours.

DAVID   You didn't.

SYD   Let it go, for the love of God!

DAVID   (*A genuine question.*) Or did you?

She doesn't reply.

Always me lookin out for you from time, weren't it. Always me lookin out for you, then sank shifted. Tables got turned.

SYD   That's life. High times, low times. Mustn't dwell.

DAVID	If I weren't such a fuck-up, you wouldn't know what to do.
SYD	So, *I'm* the problem, am I?
DAVID	Did I say –
SYD	*I'm* somehow the obstacle preventin you from leading this theoretical better life in which you ain't a delusional gay narcissist?
DAVID	If the past made me that maybe it's time to admit it's made you things too.
SYD	What you wafflin about?
DAVID	You do have a tendency to play mother.
SYD	(*Guffawing.*) Oh, pop off, sis!
DAVID	Well, ain't that why you with Jake?
SYD	You taken yer medication?
DAVID	Cos he's the only one who'll put up with it!

Pause.

SYD	(*With quiet conviction.*) I'm done, David. I try to help. God knows, I try. But you pull me down to where you are... You're right. I ain't your... I got bigger things to be thinkin about. You're on your own. (*She hangs up.*)

Scene Five

KING	(*To the cameraman, off.*) Are we good?
INTERVIEWER	I don't know. Are we good to go? (*Getting the all clear.*) Okay. Firstly – I had so much fun watching. It didn't look like you had any fun at all.
KING	(*Deadpan.*) It was dreadful. (*He quickly shoots a smile.*)
INTERVIEWER	Haha. No, but seriously. What's it like stepping into those boots again?
KING	What's it like playing Craw? Hmm. Oh, that's a good question.
	DAVID *watching* KING *from the shadows, changing into his premiere clothes.*
INTERVIEWER	When you were young did you ever imagine finding yourself at the heart of a story where you're a hero in an epic space adventure like this?
KING	(*Light and breezy.*) Did I imagine I'd be appearing in a movie like this? Probably not.
INTERVIEWER	And now you're a role model, I'm presuming that's pretty tough, no?
	KING *flashes a wry smile as* DAVID*, still watching, continues dressing.*
KING	Well, we all need a superhero, right? A friend. An ally.
INTERVIEWER	*Absolutely.* You bring up the word ally. Where do you yourself as a queer-identifying cis-gen man stand in the debate over gay artists playing gay roles?
KING	I believe representation matters. Some would say should it matter at the expense of the art, and – well – I guess that's what people who are frightened of representation say.

DAVID *stops dressing.*

I'd like to think one day we can get to the point where anyone can play anything.

INTERVIEWER But is today that day? Some might say you yourself have benefitted from being able to play *anything*. You're fluid in your own sexuality?

KING Correct.

INTERVIEWER You date men and women?

KING I have in the past, yes... That's a great shirt by the way.

INTERVIEWER Thank you. (*Smiling.*)

KING Great shirt.

INTERVIEWER There's a fashion in the entertainment industry right now for queer-baiting. Of celebrities appropriating our culture, making a lot of money and reaping the benefits, but never being fully open about who they are. What do you make of that?

KING What do I make of that?

INTERVIEWER Yes. What do you make of that?

KING (*A little flustered.*) Well... I believe we all have a right to a personal life, famous or not.

INTERVIEWER Even if you present to the community as an LGBTQIA+ advocate?

KING I presume you're referring to me.

INTERVIEWER I'm referring to queer identifying celebrities who wave the flag but who remain, well, curiously private about their own existence. There's no denying you are private about a certain aspect of your life.

KING I am private. (*Cheekily.*) I am totally the most boring man that exists. There really is nothin for the world to know.

INTERVIEWER   And apart from you being queer there is
               nothing the world does know.

               KING *looks at him for a moment, swallows,*
               then smiles.

KING   I made a plan for myself comin into this
               business as a young kid to look after me.
               (*With complete rigour and conviction.*) I don't
               feel the need to share myself with anyone.
               I don't want to share my family, my partners,
               my nieces or nephews or any of that crap.
               I don't want it. I can't be more truthful than
               that. It's always been a part of my plan to live
               the life my ancestors couldn't. That many
               a black man couldn't. And in order to do that
               I had to press mute on all the noise, the
               nonsense, the chatter. This moment, the
               connections we're making, that's all I'm
               really interested in. Connections. Stayin
               present in the now. (*With a disarming*
               warmth.) That's the reason I'm here enjoying
               talking to people like your good self, because
               I believe in the message of Craw. There are
               people for who these films can be of great
               value, not just our allies.

INTERVIEWER   Absolutely. Though don't you think little
               queer kids out there may benefit from seeing
               their black superhero visibly embrace his
               queerness?

KING   I really don't see how my standing on a red
               carpet holding hands with whoever I'm dating
               is gonna stop a kid from getting their head
               flushed down a toilet.

INTERVIEWER   So you *are* dating?

KING   (*Playing along.*) Very good.

INTERVIEWER   There's been a lot of speculation these last
               days about your romantic life.

KING   Has there?

INTERVIEWER Well... Let's see. Er... (*Reading from his notes*.) You were recently photographed arm in arm with the twenty-two-year-old rapper-slash-musician, Don Richards. There are rumours swirling around the internet that you are indeed married but have now left the marital home. There are also numerous accounts online of sexual escapades at a nightclub in Clapham last spring. When do you get the chance to dry-clean that cape?

KING *doesn't reply.*

You seem kind of angry.

KING   Is that what you'd like me to be?

INTERVIEWER Not at all. I'd like you to be honest. I think your fans would also like that. For you to be honest.

KING *doesn't answer.*

Why you looking at me like that?

KING   Like what?

INTERVIEWER I don't know. Like...

KING   I'm just waiting for you to ask your question.

Pause.

INTERVIEWER What kind of queer are you?

Scene Six

RAHEEM	Is that what you're wearin?
DAVID	Why you 'ere?
RAHEEM	I wanted to show my support.
DAVID	*I'm* the support.
RAHEEM	The King messaged at the weekend, said he could get a free flight.

RAHEEM *immediately checks himself out in the mirror.*

I saw the pictures. This is peak, bruv. It's all the Twitter gays are talkin about. One guy says he already knew King was a slag cos he sucked off their friend in a nightclub in Clapham before they even opened the marriage! Clapham gays are the worst.

JACKSON *enters with* DAVID's *jacket.*

JACKSON	King's delayed and Stevie's stuck in Dubai. He won't make it till tomorrow.

He gives DAVID *the jacket.* DAVID *puts it on.* RAHEEM *looks at* JACKSON *and smiles.*

RAHEEM	Hi.
JACKSON	Hey.
DAVID	Jackson, this is Raheem. Raheem's dating a French man.
RAHEEM	(*Quickly interjecting, shaking his hand.*) *Was* dating a French man. We broke up.
JACKSON	You must lift… I asked them to send up King's drinks order. It's all on the studio's expense account, so just – whack down whatever.
RAHEEM	(*Grinning flirtatiously.*) I'll be sure to do that.

JACKSON *smiles.*

I'm gonna go freshen up.

RAHEEM *leaves.*

JACKSON   Sorry, we haven't had a chance to dry-clean it.

A beat.

Bummer about Stevie. I was looking forward to meeting him finally. A travel writer. Sounds exotic... You can always tell a lot by who someone chooses to be with. (*Of the jacket.*) It's not too small?

DAVID   It's fine.

JACKSON   What's Stevie like?

DAVID   Hard to describe.

JACKSON   Try me.

DAVID   Pale... Gaunt... Sallow skin. Incredibly tired eyes.

JACKSON   Sounds a catch.

JACKSON *smiles, which has the effect of annoying* DAVID *greatly.*

Do you reckon they'll divorce? The photos were pretty damning.

DAVID   King told you about their marriage?

JACKSON   I work in PR. It's my job to know everything.

A beat.

Polyamorists, they're like the billionaires of romance, most of us can't get one boyfriend, they get several, ha?

DAVID   What makes you assume King has several?

JACKSON   Like I said, I work in PR. I sensed things weren't quite right on the last film. We got to

know each other pretty well on *Crawtopia*...
This one night we all got completely blottoed.
Crawled up to Bondi Rocks and jumped into
the ocean naked. I got stung by a jellyfish.
King stood over me with his cock in his hand
and he pissed on me.

JACKSON *smiles at the memory.*

He pissed on me to remove the sting.
Jellyfish. Such little mites.

He laughs a little. Then –

If you need anything I'll be working in the
next room.

JACKSON *goes.* DAVID *waits. He goes to
the mirror and unsuccessfully tries to button
the jacket. He smells the lapel, turns and sees*
ROOM SERVICE *stood there with the drinks.*

DAVID   Oh, that's for my friend. Just put it down over
there.

ROOM SERVICE *places down the tray and
stares at* DAVID *who stares back. A beat.*

He ain't 'ere.

ROOM SERVICE *looks at him. They go.
Music from next door. Something like 'My
High' by Disclosure & Slowthai. People
laughing in the next room.* DAVID *turns and
looks at the drinks tray. Slowly, he goes over,
picks up a bottle and pours. The music fills
the space.*

Scene Seven

The music pulsates. Every time DAVID *takes another drink from a* WAITER *represents another jump forward in time.*

RAHEEM   Yo, yo. One o'clock. No, no don't, don't turn your head. Okay. Slowly, slowly turn your head.

                They do.

                If I was ten years younger I'd gladly rearrange his guts.

DAVID   I thought you were tryin monogamy.

RAHEEM   And I thought you didn't drink. Where'd you go?

DAVID   To request a song.

RAHEEM   That dress. All she needs is a wand... Fuck. She's seen me. Don't move.

                He goes off. DAVID *takes a shot from a* WAITER. *The music becomes deafening.* JACKSON *appears.*

JACKSON   ARE YOU OKAY?

DAVID   WHAT?

JACKSON   I SAID ARE YOU OKAY?

DAVID   WHERE'S KING?

JACKSON   ON THE ROOF.

                A beat.

                THE SHOULDER OF YOUR WAISTCOAT.

                JACKSON *goes.* DAVID *touches the shoulder of the waistcoat, feels the rip. He takes another drink from a* WAITER. *He sips. He turns.*

KWEKU   If it isn't my favourite victim.

DAVID	You seen King up 'ere?
KWEKU	(*Noticing the drink in* DAVID*'s hand.*) ...Your boy tonight blew their socks off.

DAVID *doesn't reply.* KWEKU *smiles.*

Y'know, lot of people don't like what we do.
They think we're providing the public with
the artistic equivalent of a hamburger...
You've a hole in your vest.

DAVID *doesn't respond.* KWEKU *smiles.*

I bet secretly you'd *love* to watch me get it
on, ha?

DAVID	I'd rather fuck a pillow.
KWEKU	Ha! Enjoy your night.

He goes, off. A beat. DAVID *takes another
drink from a* WAITER. RAHEEM *appears.*

DAVID	That guy asked in the toilets if I had more paper towels. He thought I was the help.
RAHEEM	Ha! What'd I say before we left? If you wear the waistcoat *and* the bow tie ya gotta wear the jacket, or this whole motif it's just... it's *very* Forest Whitaker in *The Butler.*

I skipped a leg day for this.

DAVID	If you concentrated on actin as much as you do your body, you could be Meryl.
RAHEEM	Oh, fuck off Uta Hagen and drink your juice... Where ya goin?
DAVID	Back downstairs.
RAHEEM	(*As he goes.*) If you see King tell him I'm up 'ere.

A HOST *stands there clutching a walkie-
talkie and a list. Australian.*

HOST	Surname?
DAVID	Fairclough.
HOST	Name of the party?
DAVID	King Grant.
HOST	King Grant as in Craw?
DAVID	Yeah.

She looks him up and down.

HOST	Wristband?
DAVID	Weren't give one.
HOST	Then I'm afraid I can't let you in.
DAVID	Look, I can call him but there's no reception.
HOST	You can get reception upstairs. Step aside please, sir.
DAVID	But –
HOST	To one side. We've people waiting.

DAVID *looks at her, turns, rubs his eye and under his breath says –*

DAVID	Fuckin bitch.
HOST	…Excuse me?
DAVID	Wha's that?
HOST	You called me a bitch.
DAVID	No. No, I said *this* is a bitch. As in this situation… I didn't call *you* a bitch.

She steps towards him.

HOST	Listen –
KING	He's with me.

KING *steps out of the shadow in a white suit.* HOST *looks at them and leaves.*

Why you drinkin?

DAVID	Why's anyone drink?... (*From* KING'*s look.*) Don't look at me like that.
KING	Like what?
DAVID	Like yer my father and I've upset you.
	KING *looks away.*
KING	Someone said tonight you must feel lucky.
DAVID	Well... You've got your own doll.
KING	They think it's bold and brave puttin me in a superhero film.
DAVID	It is.
KING	That's like the dumbest shit I ever heard you say. Bold and brave would be a queer black superhero fightin for the rights of gays in countries where they'll throw you off a buildin simply for being gay. That'd be real brave, right? Instead I'm trapped. Talced into the costume, talced out of it. Fetishised for being this palatable version of what they think a black superhero is. I tell them I've nothin to say about my sexuality, I'm not queer enough. I've nothin to say about my race, I wanna let the work speak for itself, I'm not black enough. If I've too much ambition and question my own people, I'm uppity or tryna be white. And I have to hold that. I have to hold *all* of it. It's like I can't find any connection to this thing they need me to be. The longer I do these films it's like I'm sinkin in all this weird Christian dogma. The same dogma I spent years as a kid tryna escape. I mean, I don't wanna do this shit. I went to Juilliard for fuck's sake.
DAVID	The film's really not that bad.
KING	No, it's worse than bad. It's fuckin terrible.
	A moment of hesitation, then –
	And then there's Stevie.

DAVID	What about him?
KING	The whole deal was if we do this it stayed between us. If I come clean about everyone I've… I lose him. And if I don't go public I'm judged by my own community for something that's literally no one's God damn fuckin business! They don't own me. I own me… And yet…
	KING *looks away.*
DAVID	Dance with me.
KING	Now's not the time.
DAVID	(*Excitedly, clutching at his arm.*) They're playin our song.
KING	Later. (*Trying to disentangle himself from* DAVID.)
DAVID	(*Clutching further at him.*) Come!
KING	David! No. No, David!
	He pulls away but DAVID *doesn't let go.* DAVID*'s drink spills over him.*
	Fuck.
	RAHEEM *appears.*
RAHEEM	Finally.
	KING *barges past him and goes off.* RAHEEM *looks to* DAVID *confused.*
	What the fuck?
	DAVID *looks away.*
	You didn't have to borrow one of his suits, we coulda easily bought you one.
	JACKSON *appears.*
JACKSON	Where's the King?
RAHEEM	Probably tryna get his card stamped before the Queen Consort comes.

JACKSON	Who?
RAHEEM	Stevie.

A beat. RAHEEM *looks at* JACKSON.

How far away do you live?

JACKSON	Not far. Why?
RAHEEM	I think we should go there.
JACKSON	…I'll get my coat.

JACKSON *goes*. RAHEEM *looks at* DAVID.
He leaves. DAVID *looks out at* KING *with
the* WAITER. *He suddenly undoes his bow tie
and the top button of his shirt. He takes a
tissue from his pocket, wipes the sweat from
his brow and takes a drink from a* WAITER.
KWEKU *appears out of the shadow, smoking*.

KWEKU	Jackie Wilson, that's who you remind me of.

DAVID *turns, notices him. Then looks away.*

You don't like me much.

DAVID	That makes no sense. I don't know you.
KWEKU	Would you care to?

DAVID *doesn't answer.*

People love to come after the successful black
man.

KWEKU *drinks*.

You know why people like your friend? Cos
he's likeable. Most people aren't. (*He inhales*.)
I never met a person my entire life I could say
I wanna marry. I didn't wanna marry my wife,
but I did. I didn't wanna marry a lotta people.
But I'd marry King.

DAVID	Yer tellin me you're gay for King now, is
that it?

KWEKU	I'm not gay, David. I'm a straight man who does gay things.

He looks at DAVID.

That was a joke, millennial… Eighteen years I been married. Infatuation doesn't last forever. The hoax is monogamy can actually happen.

DAVID   Why you tellin me this?

KWEKU   Cos you've a Herculean knack of making people feel bad. Plus my analyst said the things you're afraid to talk about turn out to be the things that destroy you. He also said if you talk about them, as painful as they are, you might help make them go away.

DAVID   And what if it only makes things worse?

KWEKU *brings the cigarette to* DAVID*'s mouth.* DAVID *inhales.*

Scene Eight

KWEKU *gives* DAVID *the cigarette as he chops the coke.* DAVID *removes his waistcoat.*

KWEKU   You're handsome, y'know that? Your King doesn't deserve you.

He does a line then passes the note to DAVID, *who snorts.* KWEKU *takes back his cigarette, he hands* DAVID *a glass of wine.*

Tell me somethin. Your favourite superhero growin up?

DAVID   Didn't 'ave one.

KWEKU   Everyone gotta have at least one favourite superhero.

DAVID says nothing, drinks the wine.
KWEKU looks at him.

Y'know, if you wasn't makin my dick so hard right now I'd ask you to leave.

DAVID   You want me to go?

KWEKU doesn't answer. DAVID takes
KWEKU's hand and inhales on the cigarette.

KWEKU   Green Lantern. My favourite superhero, it was Green Lantern.

DAVID   Bathroom?

KWEKU points. DAVID hands him his wine,
he goes off. KWEKU stubs out the cigarette.

KWEKU   Green Lantern's whole thing was willpower. Like if he stopped believing he ceased to function. So... in order to function he always had to believe.

He sits on the bed, puts down the glass, takes
off his shoes and massages his feet.

The most interesting moments were when he fails to do this... He taps into our doubts... It's why people like Craw. Most superheroes come and know they need to save the day. Whereas Craw's always strugglin a little.

The light flickers on and off. KWEKU stares
up. A toilet flush. He puts on music.
Something like 'Can You Get to That', by
Funkadelic. DAVID enters. KWEKU picks up
the wine and hands it to DAVID.

DAVID   (*Suddenly looking at him.*) You remind me of my old man.

KWEKU   What's that, is that a compliment?

DAVID shrugs. The lights flicker on and off
again. They look up. They laugh. They drink.

What was he like?

DAVID   …The kinda man who'd punch you in the
                   face, but cry listenin to Sade.

KWEKU   Whoa! Sounds kinda hot…

                   They drink.

                   Why'd he punch you?

DAVID   (*Wiping his mouth.*) …I'd answer back.

KWEKU   (*Disingenuously.*) You?

DAVID   I'd steal stuff.

KWEKU   Go on.

DAVID   …Sometimes I'd refuse to eat me dinner.

KWEKU   What else?

DAVID   I'd – I'd throw stones at the kids who'd call
                   my sister and I a wog.

                   DAVID *takes another line. He wipes his nose.*

KWEKU   What did he do, your old man? What was his
                   job?

DAVID   Karate instructor.

KWEKU   (*Suddenly impressed.*) You know karate? No
                   way. Get out! We should do some. We should
                   do some karate, right now, legit. You any good?

DAVID   No.

KWEKU   He didn't teach you?

DAVID   He tried… He wanted me to be a man.

KWEKU   You are a man, aren't you?

                   A beat.

DAVID   Changin rooms were pretty cool. All them
                   willies.

                   KWEKU *laughs. He goes over and snorts
                   a line.*

This one time he was in the showers. I was sat waitin. All these naked grown-arse men hittin each other with towels.

KWEKU   You get a boner?

DAVID   Mm.

KWEKU *sits on the bed beside him.*

They all left. Me dad's sports bag it was open. He was still in the showers. He'd use the steam room first. Liked to keep himself real nice. I put my hand inside the bag.

KWEKU   Because you wanted to steal somethin?

DAVID   No. Because I wanted to find out who he was. He was a mystery, see. *All* men were a mystery. Still are. I rummaged through – found this pack of playin cards. Not any old playin cards, oh no. These were pornographic playin cards. I took em out their box, had a peek. Never seen anythin like it my whole life. There were women bein pummelled by men. I'm talkin two-on-one. One-on-three. All these cocks.

KWEKU   Where?

DAVID   Everywhere! There were cocks in hands, cocks in arses. Cocks up cunts, in mouths and in arses. Cocks every place imaginable. These men they were holdin em, strokin em, rubbin, wankin, milkin, suckin. It was like a PowerPoint presentation on cock, ya get me. And I was only nine years old, you understand. Everythin I learnt about what a cock could do I learnt from that pack of playin cards.

KWEKU, *greatly amused, inhales.* KWEKU *holds his hand out,* DAVID *holds it, inhales too.*

KWEKU   (*Lighting another cigarette.*) That's quite
               a hot story.

DAVID   Oh, it don't end there. I put one in me pocket.
               Took it to school to show the other kids. The
               lads in my class paid me in their lunch money
               for the privilege of seein it.

KWEKU   (*Laughing.*) Good boy.

DAVID   I made five whole pounds. When I got to ten
               I was gunna buy this really snazzy collection
               of Dorling Kindersley encyclopedias I'd seen
               in the window down at Woolies. But, well...

KWEKU   What? What happened next?

DAVID   One of the parents phoned the school,
               reported me. Said we had a pervert in our
               midst. I got summoned to the head teacher's
               office. She demanded I hand over the playin
               card. I didn't know what she was talkin about,
               but she persisted. I made up this story. I found
               it on the way to school. I wanted to protect
               my dad. She told me if I didn't hand it over
               she'd call me parents. I handed it over and she
               called em anyway. Said I was depraved. Mum
               and Dad came up the school and I waited for
               em outside that office while Mrs Welthorpe
               showed em this plastic laminated card of two
               hot niggas spit-roastin this woman who kinda
               looked like Cybill Shepherd.

               KWEKU *laughs and drinks.*

               We drove home in silence. When we got in
               I went straight to me room. I knew what was
               comin. Not that I was prepared. I jus remember
               wishin, prayin I could disappear. Wantin to be
               invisible. If I coulda chosen a superpower in
               that moment I woulda chosen to be invisible.
               Cos then he shuts the door, draws the curtains
               and tells me to take off my clothes. And even
               though it's 'appened many times before, and

even though it's 'appened to him, and his
father before him, and his father before that,
I somehow know this time'll be worse. This
time'll be his greatest performance. The thing
that makes me a man. And I am ready. Ready
to take all he has. Secretly I even want it.
I want it because I'm bad. I was born bad...
I close my eyes. Sound of leather bein pulled
from cotton. Breathe in, he begins. He begins
to thrash me. He begins to thrash me till I can't
stand. Till I can no longer walk. Till my voice
evaporates and I scream myself to silence. He
thrashes my back, he thrashes my legs, my
arms. Even thrashes the soles of my feet. Only
part of me he don't touch is my face, cos I'm
curled up into this ball, tighter than tight and he
can't reach me. After he's finished he puts back
on his belt. I'm cryin, shakin. I see the
appendix scar on his waist, the one he said was
a knife wound. Says if ever I embarrass him
again next time'll be worse. I look to the door.
My sister's standin there clutchin her Care
Bear. She starts cryin. He picks her up, closes
the door, leaves.

KWEKU *looks at* DAVID. *There is complete
silence, apart from the music beneath them.*

I was tryna protect him.

His thought trails off. A moment or two.
KWEKU *suddenly holds* DAVID*'s hand.
They sit like that for a while saying nothing.
Some time passes, far longer than you think.*

KWEKU   You want more coke?

DAVID   (*Turning and looking at* KWEKU.) I want
             you to fuck me.

KWEKU   (*Turning to him surprised.*) Huh?

DAVID   I want you to fuck me. Can you do that? Can
             you tell me what I should do?

KWEKU	(*Reluctantly, almost a whisper.*) Erm. Yeah. Yeah, K.
	DAVID *gets up from the bed, stands in front of him and waits.*
DAVID	Well? You gon tell me?
KWEKU	Tell you what?
DAVID	Whatever you want.
KWEKU	(*Almost laughing, going to him.*) Here. Sit. You're drunk.
DAVID	(*Fending him off.*) Nah.
	KWEKU *steps back. A long pause. He stares at DAVID hard. He puts down his wine glass.*
KWKEU	Take off your clothes.
DAVID	I need you to be more specific than that, Daddy Crawtopia.
KWEKU	(*Firmly.*) Take off *all* your clothes.
	DAVID *complies.* KWEKU *looks, puts one hand to his groin and gestures with the other.*
	There.
	He points to the open window. DAVID *goes and stands there.*
	Turn around.
	DAVID *turns to face the open window.* KWEKU *surveys him, slightly rubbing himself.*
	Who said you could look?
	DAVID *turns back round.* KWEKU *gets up, turns down the lights, puts the music back on. He removes his shirt, walks to DAVID and stands behind him. He takes DAVID's arms and lifts them, holding them outstretched. We can barely see their bodies. He moves DAVID's arms in motion as though he were*

a bird in flight. Lowering DAVID'*s arms he turns him round to face him. They embrace before* KWEKU *pushes* DAVID *down to the floor.* DAVID *fellates* KWEKU. *They kiss and move back to the bed.*

You like that, huh?

KWEKU *climbs atop* DAVID, *rubbing against him.*

Mm-hmm. That good?

Still wearing his trousers, he quickly kisses DAVID *again while thrusting against him.*

DAVID   (*Breathlessly.*) Harder.

KWEKU *pins* DAVID'*s arms to the bed.*

KWEKU   You want it?

DAVID *takes* KWEKU'*s hand and places it around his neck.*

DAVID   Yeah, put it in me.

KWEKU *suddenly stops, breaking out of it completely.*

KWEKU   What? You mean like in you in you, or –

DAVID   Yeah! In me. Tell me I'm worthless.

KWEKU *suddenly sits upright.*

What? What's the matter? You cum?

KWEKU   I'm not into that… That whole daddy–son, kinda… Can I just cum on your ass?

DAVID *looks at him with disappointment. He shrugs.*

Let me freshen up.

KWEKU *goes to the bathroom.* DAVID *lays staring at the ceiling. He scratches his pubes. A moment. He quickly bolts up and puts on his pants. A toilet flush. He looks toward the bathroom. The light above him flickers. He stares up, then back to the bathroom. DAVID sits back on the bed. Something like 'I Put a Spell on You' by Alice Smith plays from off. He stares up at the ceiling. After a while the light above him flickers on and off. Silence. Darkness. DAVID sits up. We hear footsteps approaching. A sudden blinding bright light pierces through the space. A low subterranean rumble overpowers the atmosphere, like the screeching of a train in a tunnel. It increases in volume and pitch as the music starts up again. From the direction of the bathroom CRAW suddenly flies into the room, a halo of light emanating from his silhouette. DAVID recoils back onto the bed as CRAW places his finger to his lip, for DAVID to be silent. CRAW ambles towards him, grunting like a wild feral animal. He stops at the foot of the bed, then raises both hands. A command to the gods. CRAW makes it rain sand. DAVID looks up as CRAW, now on the bed, pulls DAVID towards him, grabbing, tearing at him, DAVID tries to fight him off. There is a tussle as CRAW flips DAVID over so he is face-down. Once he has him on all-fours, with one hand CRAW undoes his fly, with the other he rips down DAVID's pants. Now exposed, DAVID's legs are forcibly spread open by CRAW while he manically tries to grip the edge of a surface, any surface to get some purchase. As CRAW enters him he closes his eyes, the stage now filling around them with sand. DAVID cries out, the blinding light pierces through the space, the music bursting as CRAW's body envelopes DAVID, dominating, taking, invading. DAVID murmurs in both pleasure and pain until CRAW finally orgasms.*

*After a moment, the sound of beating wings
mingled with the screeching jangle of iron
and metal as he grunts wildly. It is now over.*
CRAW *steps back and looks down at* DAVID
as the bed disappears into the sand. DAVID
looks around. The superhero is gone. DAVID
pulls at his pants.

Scene Nine

*Daylight. The colours in the space are now sharper, more vivid.
Something has shifted.* KING *is applying suncream. He looks
out to the sea.* DAVID *enters and sits by him. Pause.*

KING   It's so peaceful.

            KING *puts on his Ray-Bans, lays back and
            looks out. A pause.*

DAVID   I been thinkin.

            He looks back out to the sea.

            I wanna go back to how we were.

KING   What?

DAVID   I said I wanna go back to how we were. Like
            how we were before.

            Pause. KING *sits up. He takes off his
            sunglasses.*

KING   I do love you, David. You know that, right?

DAVID   And I you… Only I'm *in* love with you.

            He smiles. Noise from the beach.

            And I can't keep fallin into it. Cos I do. When
            we spend time. When I see you I fall. If I'm
            around you I lose… It's like all these parts of
            me I been tryna get right… Make sense?

They are now facing each other.

KING   Yeah.

DAVID   Well.

                    Pause.

                    My agent messaged... I got Horatio.

KING   Shut up. (*He smiles.*) That's great.

DAVID   Yeah. (*With belief.*) Yeah.

                    STEVEN *enters holding two melted ice creams. He hands one to* KING.

STEVEN   (*Taking off his flip flops and sitting.*) Did you put on that sunscreen?

                    KING *doesn't answer. The sound of children in the distance playing.*

                    Seen over there? They're moving up the beach by gradations. Your faithful army.

KING   I think it's sweet.

STEVEN   You would.

                    They eat their ice creams. STEVEN *turns to* DAVID.

                    Y'know, when we first met I thought he was shy. (*He eats.*) Then I quickly realised... shyness is a vanity. Secretly he loves the attention.

KING   (*Irritated, but being polite.*) I do *not* love the attention.

STEVEN   Oh, yes you do.

                    KING *doesn't respond.*

                    (*Generously to* DAVID.) Sure you don't want some ice cream, David? You can have some of mine.

DAVID   I'm cool.

              KING *and* STEVEN *go back to eating.*
              DAVID *stares out to the sea. The sound of*
              gulls overhead. He stares. And stares.

Scene Ten

SYD   You don't 'ave to.

DAVID   I want to.

              She looks about, holding the now-visible
              bump of her stomach.

              Still looks the same, innit.

SYD   Yeah. It's a shithole.

DAVID   ...It's alright.

SYD   Would be if everyone who lived 'ere moved.
              Lumpy white red bodies everywhere.

              They spoil the view... Wha's the time?

DAVID   (*Looking at his watch.*) Half past.

SYD   He's on black time. (*He gives her a look.*)
              What? I said to Jake I'd be back by three.

              She looks around.

              Mum used to send us over there to get her tea.
              Boilin-hot tea on a scorchin summer's day.
              Never understood it.

              She says nothing. Then –

              I'm gunna go wait in the car.

DAVID   Stay.

SYD   You want me to get a ticket?

DAVID   No. I want you to stay.

SYD *looks at him sat there like a child.*
A beat. She sits beside him.

Wha's over there?

SYD   (*Looking out.*) Canvey.

DAVID   That ain't Canvey.

SYD   Yeah it is.

DAVID   No it ain't.

SYD   It is.

DAVID   Is not. (*With certainty.*) Canvey's there.

He points. They look.

SYD   You walked all the way over there once – tide
               was out. Mum went mental. Had all the adults
               lined up on the beach signallin for ya to come
               back.

DAVID   I thought they were wavin.

SYD   I know. You waved straight back... Fuckin
               numpty.

They laugh. SYD *plays with her car keys.*

One summer there was this little boy. All his
sisters were sat on the beach head to toe in
skirts. Swelterin. They were Hasidic.
Orthodox. We were lookin at em like how do
you do it in this heat? Big thick cloth, like
that – (*She gestures with her fingers.*) You
went over. Started playin with the little boy.
Thick as thieves you were. Built sandcastles
together. Lent him your dinghy. Then the
holidays was over, so we went home. Next
year we came back and he weren't there. You
cried. Proper sobbin and shit. Hyperventilatin.
Couldn't breathe. Dad said what you cryin
for? You thought you'd never see the little
boy again. And he took you – Dad took you
into his arms and he held you. Said it's okay.

That it was all gunna be fine. Said there'd be other little boys you can play with. That that's just life. That it'll all be fine.

DAVID *says nothing*.

He came to see you – when you were in hospital. Told me not to say anythin.

He looks at her.

Fifteen years, David. He's a proud man. You both are.

Pause. He holds out his hand. She takes it. They stay that way for a bit looking out to the mudflats and coastline. A beat.

I'll get us a ticket.

SYD *leaves. The sound of gulls. A moment. He looks to his feet. He removes his trainers and socks, placing the socks inside the trainers. He puts them beside him. Silence. He looks out, feels the sun on his face. He breathes in – perhaps he closes his eyes. He waits.*

Blackout.

The End.

A Nick Hern Book

BLACK SUPERHERO first published as a paperback original in Great Britain in 2023 by Nick Hern Books Limited, The Glasshouse, 49a Goldhawk Road, London W12 8QP, in association with the Royal Court Theatre, London

Cover image: © Ajamu Ikwe-Tyehimba. All rights reserved, DACS 2023

Designed and typeset by Nick Hern Books, London
Printed in Great Britain by CPI Group (UK) Ltd

A CIP catalogue record for this book is available from the British Library

ISBN   978 1 83904 143 3